TEEN AUTISM ESSENTIALS

A STEP-BY-STEP PATH TO NAVIGATING ADOLESCENCE
AND EMOTIONAL GROWTH, PARENT AND EDUCATOR
SUPPORT, AND PREPARATION FOR ADULTHOOD AND
INDEPENDENCE

JASON JONES

TABLE OF CONTENTS

INTRODUCTION

One afternoon, Jack, a teenager with autism, stood at the edge of a busy school cafeteria. The noise was overwhelming, the chatter blending into an annoying buzz that made it hard for him to focus. But Jack had a plan. He scanned the room, looking for his friend who always saved him a spot. With a deep breath, he walked through the crowd, his anxiety subsiding with each step as he reached his destination. This small victory was a testament to Jack's growth and determination, reflecting his journey toward independence and self-advocacy.

This book is for people like Jack and the parents and educators who support them. Its purpose is to serve as a guide for teenagers with autism as they navigate the complexities of adolescence. It aims to provide practical strategies, emotional support, and self-advocacy tools. You will find insights that help make sense of the unique challenges and opportunities that come with being a teenager on the autism spectrum.

My vision for this book is to offer a fresh perspective on teenage autism. I draw from existing research, personal experience and stories, and real-life case studies. The aim is to educate, inspire, and uplift. Through these narratives, I want to create a sense of community and understanding. It's about sharing experiences and finding strength in shared journeys.

This book's primary audience includes teenagers with autism, their parents, and educators. Each group has specific needs and questions. Teenagers may wonder about fitting in and making friends. Parents might seek advice on supporting their child's emotional growth. Educators could look for strategies to create inclusive learning environments. This book speaks to each of these concerns with empathy and practical advice.

What makes this book unique is its authentic representation of autism. It offers practical advice and diverse perspectives. You'll hear voices from different backgrounds, each bringing their own insights and experiences. This diversity enriches the narrative and provides a broader understanding of autism in the teenage years.

In the coming chapters, you'll find a range of topics covered. We'll explore emotional intelligence and how to handle feelings in a healthy way. We look at self-advocacy, teaching how to speak up for oneself and communicate needs effectively. We'll also discuss preparing for adulthood, focusing on skills that promote independence and confidence. Each chapter builds on the last, creating a comprehensive roadmap for navigating adolescence with autism.

My connection to this subject is deeply personal. I was just diagnosed with autism a few years ago, so I went through my teenage years not knowing that I had autism, but I always felt like I didn't quite fit in with any of the groups or clicks at school. I also moved a lot as a kid and went to three different high schools. So, not only did I get to be the "new kid" three times, I did this with undiagnosed autism. I have seen the challenges and triumphs firsthand

and am committed to sharing what I've learned to help others on their journey.

As you read this book, I encourage you to engage with the content actively and apply what you learn to your own life or the lives of those you support.

The key takeaway from this introduction is one of hope and practicality. The journey through adolescence is complex, especially for those on the autism spectrum. However, with the proper knowledge, it is possible to work through these complexities successfully. This book aims to equip you with those resources.

1

UNDERSTANDING AUTISM IN ADOLESCENCE

Have you ever met a teenager who could recite every type of dinosaur that roamed the Earth, complete with Latin names and dietary habits? Meet Emily, a 14-year-old with autism whose fascination with paleontology rivals that of a seasoned archaeologist. She has transformed her room into a mini-museum, complete with a fossil replica collection. Her knowledge is impressive, and her passion is incredible. However, Emily's social interactions at school can feel like walking through a minefield. While she is comfortable when discussing her interests, casual hallway chats can be terrifying. Emily's story is just one example of the diversity within the autism spectrum and illustrates the unique challenges and triumphs faced by autistic teens as they navigate adolescence.

THE SPECTRUM UNVEILED: DIVERSITY IN TEENAGE AUTISM

Autism, often referred to as Autism Spectrum Disorder (ASD), is a developmental condition that influences how a person perceives the world and interacts with others. It's called a "spectrum" for a reason—no two individuals with autism are the same, and each person's experience is unique. This diversity is particularly pronounced during the teenage years, a time when everyone is trying to figure out who they are. For teens with autism, varied social skills can mean that some might excel in structured environments with clear social rules. In contrast, others might feel more comfortable engaging with peers who share their particular interests.

Differences in communication styles are also noteworthy. Some teens might be more verbal, using language to express themselves, while others might prefer non-verbal methods, like art or music, to communicate their thoughts and feelings. Then, there are unique interests and talents, like Emily's love for dinosaurs, which can become a significant part of their identity and a source of joy and self-esteem.

Adolescence is a challenging time for most, but for teenagers with autism, the complexities are often magnified. This period of life is marked by identity exploration, where teens are trying to answer the age-old question, "Who am I?" For teens with autism, this exploration can be both exciting and overwhelming. They may find comfort in deepening their understanding of their special interests, which can offer a stable sense of identity amidst the chaos of adolescence. However, peer acceptance can be a double-edged sword. While some peers may appreciate their unique perspectives and talents, others might not understand their differences, leading to feelings of isolation or exclusion. Getting through these social complexities requires resilience and support.

Consider the case of Alex, a 16-year-old passionate about coding. In the digital realm, Alex feels in control and adept at creating worlds and solving complex problems. Yet, he feels uncomfortable and isolated during school dances or lunch breaks, where social codes are unspoken and fluid. His story illustrates the challenges of balancing social expectations with personal comfort zones.

On the other hand, there's Lily, who excels in her drama club. The structured setting of scripts and rehearsals provides a framework for her to express herself freely. These examples highlight the importance of recognizing and valuing the diverse experiences of teens with autism, understanding that each has their own path to find and follow.

Given the varied needs and experiences of teens with autism, personalized approaches to support are essential. Tailored educational plans can make a significant difference, offering individualized learning strategies that play to a teen's strengths while addressing areas of challenge. These plans might include accommodations like extra time on tests or the use of technology to aid communication. Similarly, customized social skill-building activities can empower teens to develop more comfortable and effective ways to engage with peers. This might involve role-playing exercises that simulate social scenarios or joining clubs that align with their interests, providing opportunities to interact in a more structured and predictable environment.

DISCOVERING STRENGTHS AND INTERESTS

Take a moment to think about your own strengths and interests. What activities make you feel most like yourself? How can these interests become a part of your identity and help you connect with others? Write down your thoughts and consider how they might guide your path through adolescence. Whether you're a teen discovering your interests, a parent supporting your child's journey, or an educator looking to create an inclusive environment, understanding the diversity of the autism spectrum is crucial. By recognizing and celebrating these differences, we can provide the support and opportunities teens with autism need to be their best selves.

BEYOND STEREOTYPES: DEBUNKING COMMON MYTHS

Picture a young teen at a family gathering, quietly observing the interactions from the corner of the room. Someone might glance at them and assume disinterest or a lack of empathy, but that couldn't be further from the truth. A prevalent myth surrounding autism is that individuals on the spectrum lack empathy. This stereotype has been perpetuated by misunderstandings and misinterpretations of ASD behavior. In reality, many teenagers with autism experience emotions intensely and may feel deeply for others, but expressing these emotions in conventional ways can be challenging for them.

Research supports this, revealing that individuals with autism often possess the capacity for empathy but might struggle to express it due to difficulties in reading social cues or vocalizing feelings. The myth of lacking empathy overlooks these nuances, painting an inaccurate picture that can lead to social isolation and internalized stigma. To put it more simply, they feel bad because they are misunderstood.

Another common misconception concerns sensory needs. The world can be a bombardment of stimuli, and for many teens with autism, managing sensory input is a daily challenge. Yet, society often misreads this as overreaction or moodiness. Sensory sensitivities are real and can significantly impact daily life. Teens on the spectrum might find certain sounds, lights, or textures overwhelming, causing distress that others might not understand. This misunderstanding can lead to labeling, further isolating them from their peers. Sensory needs vary widely; some may seek out sensory stimuli, while others might avoid it entirely. Recognizing and respecting these needs is vital, as it creates a more inclusive environment where teens can feel understood and supported.

The impact of these stereotypes on teens with autism is profound. When society labels them as unemotional or overly sensitive, it can chip away at their self-esteem. Imagine constantly being told you don't feel or that your reactions are unwarranted. This can lead to social withdrawal and an internal belief that they are inherently different in a negative way. The weight of these stereotypes can make it difficult for teens to form meaningful connections or to feel confident in their own identity. The stigma associated with these misconceptions can prevent them from seeking out opportunities to express themselves or to engage with their peers in a way that feels genuine.

Scientific insights help counter these myths, providing a clearer picture of the autism experience. Studies have shown that individuals with autism often have a strong capacity for empathy but express it in ways that might not align with societal expectations. For instance, rather than offering verbal condolences, they might show empathy through acts of service or by sharing a favorite interest. It's important to broaden our understanding of empathy to include these diverse expressions. Similarly, recognizing the variability in sensory profiles is key. Not all teens on the spectrum will react the same way to sensory input; some might need a quiet space to decompress, while others might love environments filled with stimulating colors and sounds. Understanding these individual differences is vital in creating supportive spaces for teens with autism.

Promoting an understanding of individual differences means acknowledging that traits and behaviors can vary significantly among teens with autism. This means appreciating that each teen has a unique way of interacting with the world. One might communicate best through written words or art, while another prefers face-to-face conversation. These varied communication preferences should be encouraged, not stifled. By recognizing and valuing these differences, we can begin to dismantle the stereotypes that have long hindered individuals on the spectrum.

EXPLORING EMPATHY

Take a moment to reflect on what empathy means to you. Consider ways you express empathy that might differ from others. How can understanding different expressions of empathy help you connect with those around you? Write down your thoughts and think about how this new understanding can change how you interact with others. This exercise can be a powerful tool for teens, parents, and educators alike, helping to bring a more inclusive and empathetic community. By challenging stereotypes and embracing the rich tapestry of experiences of people with autism, we open the door to more authentic connections and deeper understanding.

NAVIGATING PUBERTY: BIOLOGICAL AND EMOTIONAL CHANGES

Ah, puberty—the great equalizer of awkwardness, confusion, and self-discovery. Now, imagine adding an extra layer of complexity to this universally challenging phase: autism. For teens on the spectrum, puberty can feel like a rollercoaster of changes, both seen and unseen. Hormonal fluctuations can wreak havoc, amplifying sensory sensitivities that might already be present. Sudden growth spurts, acne outbreaks, and voice changes are just the tip of the iceberg. These physical developments can feel overwhelming for any teen, even more so when accompanied by a brain that's already wired for intensity. It's not uncommon for teens with autism to experience these changes as amplified versions of what their neurotypical peers might feel—sort of like living life with the volume turned up.

Emotionally, puberty can introduce a whole new set of challenges. Anxiety levels might rise as social expectations and self-awareness increase. The world starts to feel like a more complicated place, where understanding oneself is as complex as understanding others. Emotional regulation, already a tricky skill, can become even more elusive. What once was a mild annoyance might now trigger an emotional outburst. Managing these emotions is crucial, yet it's often tested during this time. For many teens on the spectrum, these emotional changes can lead to feeling out of control, which is both frustrating and exhausting. Navigating these waters requires patience, understanding, and strategies to help manage this emotional upheaval.

Tailored support becomes indispensable during puberty. Sex education, for example, needs to be specific, sensitive, and inclusive of ASD needs. Understanding the mechanics of puberty is one thing; grasping the social and emotional nuances is another. Educators and parents should provide clear, direct explanations, avoiding euphemisms that might cause confusion. Support groups can also be a lifeline—not just for teens but for parents, too. These groups offer a safe space to share experiences, ask questions, and find reassurance that they're not alone in this. The shared knowledge and mutual understanding can ease anxieties, making the transition a little smoother for everyone involved.

Practical tips for guiding teens with autism through puberty are crucial. One effective method is maintaining open lines of communication. Encourage discussions about changes and feelings, even if it feels awkward. The goal is to create an environment where teens feel comfortable voicing concerns and asking questions. Consistent routines can also provide a much-needed sense of stability. Adolescence is already a time of flux, so having predictable patterns can help anchor teens during the chaos. This might include setting regular schedules for meals, homework, and leisure activities, which helps reduce stress and anxiety. Expectations should be clear and consistent, offering a framework that teens can rely on when everything else feels uncertain.

For educators, understanding the intersection of autism and puberty means being prepared to make accommodations both in and out of the classroom. Flexibility is key. Some teens may need extra time or alternative ways to complete assignments, especially when hormonal changes impact concentration or energy levels. It is also helpful to have a designated quiet space where students can retreat if they feel overwhelmed. This kind of support shows understanding and respect for the unique challenges teens on the spectrum face during puberty. Teachers should also encourage peer support, creating a classroom culture where differences are accepted and celebrated rather than criticized.

Handling puberty with autism is a complicated challenge that requires understanding and compassion. The aim should be to recognize the unique ways in which these changes unfold and find strategies to support teens through them. By addressing both the biological and emotional aspects and providing individualized resources and environments, we can help ease this transition. It's not about eliminating the challenges but equipping teens with everything they need to face them with confidence and resilience. The goal is to support teens as they continue to grow into their identities, providing them with the guidance and understanding they deserve in this pivotal time of life.

SENSORY SENSITIVITIES: RECOGNIZING AND MANAGING OVERLOAD

Imagine walking into a room where the lights are glaringly bright, a roar of sounds assaults your ears, and every fabric you touch feels like sandpaper against your skin. For some teens with autism, this isn't just an occasional experience—it's a daily reality. Sensory processing differences mean that their brains interpret sensory information in ways that can be overwhelming or even painful. This isn't a mere preference for quieter settings; it's a fundamental way their nervous system responds to stimuli.

Hyper-sensitivity might cause them to find certain noises unbearable, while hypo-sensitivity could mean they need intense stimuli to feel engaged. Both experiences shape their interactions with the world.

Let's talk about some common sensory triggers that can instantly send a teen on the spectrum from calm to overwhelmed. Loud noises, like the unexpected screech of a fire alarm or the constant hum of a crowded cafeteria, can feel like an assault on the senses, leading to heightened stress or anxiety. Bright lights, such as the harsh fluorescents in school hallways, can be equally unsettling, creating a visual overload that makes concentration nearly impossible. Even everyday sensations, like the texture of a particular fabric or the smell of a strong perfume, can trigger discomfort or distress. These sensory experiences aren't just minor annoyances; they can significantly impact a teen's ability to function in their environment.

So, what can be done to help manage these sensory sensitivities? Creating sensory-friendly spaces is a good starting point. Whether at home or school, having a designated area where the environment is tailored to reduce sensory overload can make a world of difference. This might mean using soft lighting, providing quiet corners, or allowing the use of noise-canceling headphones to block out disruptive sounds. These practical solutions help create a safe haven where teens can retreat when sensory input becomes too much to handle. Giving them control over their environment in a comfortable and manageable way can make all the difference in the world.

The importance of making sensory accommodations cannot be overstated. In a classroom setting, this might involve allowing sensory breaks, where a student can step out to a quiet space to regroup before rejoining the class. Flexible seating options, such as allowing a student to sit on a beanbag rather than a traditional chair, can also make the learning environment more accommodating. These adjustments are not about giving special treatment; they're about providing the necessary tools for teens on the spectrum to succeed on their own terms. Recognizing and respecting these needs promotes an inclusive environment that values diversity and supports individual well-being.

DISCOVER YOUR SENSORY PREFERENCES

Take a moment to think about your own sensory preferences. Are there certain sounds, sights, or textures that you find particularly soothing or irritating? Consider how these preferences affect your daily life and interactions. Write down your observations and think about ways to create sensory-friendly environments catering to your needs. This exercise can help teens on the spectrum and parents and educators better understand the importance of sensory accommodations. By embracing these differences and making thoughtful adjustments, we can help teens feel more comfortable and confident in their surroundings.

THE EMOTIONAL LANDSCAPE: UNDERSTANDING MELTDOWNS AND SHUTDOWNS

In the lively world of teenage life, emotions often run high, and for teens with autism, these emotions can sometimes feel like an untamed river, unpredictable and overwhelming. Two particular responses that arise from this emotional intensity are meltdowns and shutdowns, each distinct yet coming from the same reasons: stress and overstimulation. Picture a meltdown as a volcanic eruption, where the pressure builds until it finds an explosive release. This reaction often occurs when a teen encounters overwhelming stress, whether from sensory overload, social anxiety, or unexpected changes. A meltdown is a body's natural response to an overflow of emotions, a desperate attempt to release the tension that has built up.

On the other hand, a shutdown might be likened to a turtle retreating into its shell, withdrawing from the chaos of the world. While a meltdown is outward and explosive, a shutdown is inward and silent. It's a protective mechanism for teens to temporarily disconnect themselves from further stress. This withdrawal can manifest as an inability to talk, move, or engage with their surroundings as if the system has shut down to prevent damage. Both responses are natural, albeit challenging, and they require understanding and support from those around them.

Recognizing the triggers and signs of meltdowns and shutdowns is crucial for providing effective support. Environmental stressors like crowded spaces, loud noises, or sudden changes in routine can all spark these responses. Emotional overload, such as feeling misunderstood or facing high expectations, can also play a significant role. Early warning signs might include irritability, restlessness, or a sudden change in demeanor. By identifying these signs early, we can take proactive steps to help manage the situation before it escalates.

Managing these emotional responses involves a combination of strategies tailored to the individual's needs. De-escalation techniques, such as speaking in a calm and soothing voice, can help reduce the intensity of a meltdown. Offering a safe space for the teen to retreat to—a quiet room, a cozy corner, or even a favorite spot outside—can provide a sanctuary where they can process their emotions without external pressures. Creating an environment where the teen feels secure and in control is important, minimizing the stimuli that contribute to their distress.

Equally important is building emotional literacy, a skill that empowers teens to recognize and articulate their emotions. Teaching teens to identify their feelings—whether through emotion identification exercises, visual emotion charts, or even simple conversations—can give them the vocabulary and confidence to express themselves.

Journaling is another powerful tool, offering a private outlet for self-expression that can help clarify thoughts and feelings. By encouraging these practices, we help teens build resilience and a deeper understanding of their emotional landscape.

In this process, patience is key. Supporting teens with autism through meltdowns and shutdowns requires empathy and an open heart. The main thing is just being there, offering comfort without judgment, and understanding that these responses are not intentional but rather a part of how they navigate the world. Remember, every teen is different, and what works for one might not work for another.

The emotional landscape of a teen on the spectrum is complex, filled with peaks and valleys that can seem overwhelming and scary. Yet, with the right preparation and understanding, these challenges can become opportunities for growth and connection.

2

BUILDING EMOTIONAL INTELLIGENCE AND SELF-ADVOCACY

Imagine standing in front of a mirror, watching as your reflection morphs with each flicker of emotion across your face. You see joy, frustration, curiosity—all expressions that bubble up from the depths within. Now, imagine trying to describe these feelings with words. For many teens with autism, this task can be as puzzling as deciphering a foreign language. Yet, emotional awareness is crucial for personal development. It's the foundation for understanding oneself and building meaningful connections with others. This chapter aims to equip you with the items needed to identify, understand, and communicate your emotions effectively, paving the way for growth and self-advocacy.

Emotional awareness starts with vocabulary. Just as a painter needs a palette of colors to create a masterpiece, you need a diverse set of words to express the variety of emotions you experience. Building an emotional vocabulary lets you pinpoint feelings like a detective solving a mystery. You're no longer just "sad" or "happy"; you can articulate nuances like "anxious" or "content." Mood charts are a fantastic tool for tracking your emotional states over time. By writing down your feelings daily, you visualize your emotions, spot patterns, and gain insights into your triggers and joys. Apps for mood tracking can also offer interactive ways to log emotions, providing feedback and suggestions to improve emotional well-being.

Emotion wheels can be incredibly helpful in further identifying emotions. These colorful diagrams break down complex feelings into more manageable parts, allowing you to explore the intricacies of your emotional landscape. With a quick glance, you can trace your feelings from broad categories like "fear" or "joy" to more specific emotions such as "nervousness" or "elation." This clarity helps you understand and articulate your feelings, serving as a stepping stone toward effective communication.

Once you've identified your emotions, the next step is learning to communicate them effectively. This is where I-statements come into play. These simple yet powerful phrases frame your feelings in a way that emphasizes personal experience rather than blame. Instead of saying, "You make me angry," you could express, "I feel upset when..." This shift clarifies your emotions and develops healthier communication with others. Practicing role-playing scenarios can also enhance your ability to express feelings. By simulating conversations in a safe environment, you build confidence and refine your communication skills, preparing you for real-life interactions.

However, expressing emotions isn't always straightforward. Many teens on the spectrum face barriers that make this process challenging. Fear of judgment is a common obstacle. The worry that others might not understand or accept your feelings can be worrying, leading to hesitation or even silence. Additionally, verbalizing complex emotions can feel like untangling a knot of thoughts and sensations. It's important to acknowledge and approach these challenges with patience and empathy. You can gradually overcome these hurdles by creating supportive environments where expressing emotions is encouraged.

DEVELOPING EMPATHY: UNDERSTANDING OTHERS' PERSPECTIVES

As we mentioned earlier, empathy is the ability to understand and share the feelings of another. Empathy is like a bridge that connects us to the experiences of those around us. It's the difference between merely hearing someone and genuinely listening to them. Empathy allows you to walk in another person's shoes, even if just for a moment, and it is a powerful tool for building connections. Active listening is a key component here. It means giving your full attention when someone speaks, not just waiting for your turn to talk. By actively listening, you acknowledge the speaker's feelings and validate their experiences, making them feel seen and heard.

One effective method to develop empathy is through perspective-taking exercises. These activities encourage you to view situations from another person's point of view. For instance, you might consider how a classmate feels when they're left out of a group project or how a sibling feels after a tough day at school. Story-based empathy discussions can also help. By reading or hearing stories about diverse experiences, you can practice imagining how the characters feel and why they behave the way they do. These exercises are engaging and invaluable in developing a deeper understanding of the complex emotional landscapes of those around you.

Developing empathy, however, comes with its own set of challenges, especially for autistic teens. One of the hurdles is the difficulty in reading non-verbal cues. Facial expressions, body language, and tone of voice can convey emotions that words don't always express. Understanding these subtle signals requires practice and patience. And sometimes, the emotional responses of others might seem unpredictable or confusing, adding another layer of complexity to social interactions. Recognizing these challenges is the first step to addressing them, and seeking out opportunities to practice can help.

Empathy acts like glue in relationships, holding people together through shared understanding and compassion. It's crucial for building trust with peers. When you show empathy, you demonstrate that you care about another person's feelings and perspectives, which helps establish a foundation of trust. This trust is essential in resolving conflicts. When disagreements arise, empathy allows you to see beyond your own perspective and consider the other person's viewpoint, paving the way for compromise and mutual understanding. Conflict resolution techniques often emphasize empathy as a core component, encouraging you to listen, validate, and respond thoughtfully to the emotions of others.

Encouraging empathy requires creating environments where these skills can be nurtured. Teachers and parents can facilitate this by inviting open discussions about feelings and relationships. Role-playing different scenarios or discussing characters' emotions in books and films can be effective ways to practice empathy in a safe and controlled setting. By guiding teens through these exercises, adults help them develop the skills needed to navigate the social world with greater ease. By creating a space for teens on the spectrum, empathy can not only be taught but also valued and practiced regularly.

For teens with autism, developing empathy can feel like learning a new language. It takes time, effort, and a willingness to explore emotions that might initially feel foreign. But with practice, empathy becomes a powerful tool that enriches relationships and broadens one's understanding of the world. Once one recognizes that everyone has their own story, and by listening to these stories, one can connect more deeply with those around them.

THE ART OF SELF-ADVOCACY: SPEAKING UP FOR YOUR NEEDS

Picture yourself in a room full of people discussing your future, but nobody asks for your opinion. This is what life can feel like when you're unable to advocate for yourself. Self-advocacy means having the confidence and skills to express your needs and desires, especially when decisions about your life are being made. For teens on the spectrum, mastering self-advocacy is a step toward autonomy and personal empowerment. The first step is knowing what you need, from accommodations in school to understanding social cues and being able to communicate those needs effectively. Imagine a scenario where you're preparing for an Individualized Education Program (IEP) meeting. This meeting is your chance to speak up about what works for you in the classroom and what doesn't. Practicing how to articulate your thoughts ahead of time can make the actual meeting feel less intimidating. This is your moment to ensure that your educational environment is as supportive as possible and customized to your unique learning style and requirements.

Preparation is the key to being an effective self-advocate. Start by listing your needs and the reasons behind them. For example, if you need more time on tests, explain how it helps you process information better. Practice saying this out loud, possibly with a friend or family member, so you feel more comfortable when the time comes. Communicating needs to teachers or peers can be intimidating, but remember, you're the expert on yourself. Approach these conversations with clarity and confidence. A teacher might not realize that a simple change in seating can make a huge difference in your comfort level, and by voicing this, you're advocating for a better learning experience. Self-advocacy is about finding your voice and using it to shape the environment around you.

Challenges in self-advocacy are common and varied. Building the confidence to speak up is often the first hurdle. You might worry about how others react or fear your needs won't be taken seriously. This is where practice and support come in. Start small, perhaps with something less intimidating, like suggesting a new family routine at home. Gradually, these small victories will build your confidence to tackle more significant challenges. Dealing with resistance from others can also be tricky.

Sometimes, people might not understand or agree with your requests. Prepare for this by having a plan B or additional information to support your needs. Remember, self-advocacy is not about demanding but about communicating your needs clearly and respectfully.

Success stories abound, illustrating the power of self-advocacy. Consider Sarah, a college student on the spectrum who realized she needed quiet study spaces to focus effectively. By advocating for herself, she arranged for access to a private study room during exams, significantly improving her academic performance. Another example is James, who faced challenges in the workplace due to sensory sensitivities. By discussing his needs with his employer, he was able to have noise-canceling headphones approved, allowing him to work more comfortably and efficiently. These stories are about getting what you need and creating an environment where you can succeed.

Self-advocacy is a skill that grows with time and practice. It starts with understanding your own needs and progresses to confidently communicating them to others. Each step you take in advocating for yourself is a step towards greater independence and self-assurance. Whether it's in school, at home, or in the workplace, knowing how to speak up for yourself is an invaluable skill that lays the foundation for a fulfilling and independent life.

COPING MECHANISMS: STRATEGIES FOR MANAGING STRESS AND ANXIETY

Teenage years can often feel like a never-ending adventure, complete

with unexpected twists and turns. For teens with autism, these years come with an additional set of challenges that can contribute to stress and anxiety. Academic pressures often top the list, as the demands of schoolwork, exams, and meeting expectations can feel overwhelming. The weight of social expectations adds another layer of complexity. Whether it's working on friendships or trying to fit into the ever-changing social landscape, the pressure to conform can be immense. Understanding these everyday stressors is the first step in tackling them head-on.

Having an array of coping strategies can make all the difference. These strategies act like a safety net, offering support and relief when stress levels rise. One effective technique is deep breathing exercises. Focusing on your breath can calm your mind and bring your body back to a state of relaxation. Imagine slowly inhaling for a count of four, holding your breath for four, and then exhaling for four. This simple exercise can be done anywhere, anytime, to help reduce stress.

Meditation practices also offer a valuable way to center your thoughts and emotions. Setting aside just a few minutes daily to meditate can create a sense of calm and clarity that carries through even the most hectic moments. Physical activities, too, play a crucial role in stress relief. Whether it's a brisk walk, a dance session in your room, or a game of basketball with friends, moving your body releases endorphins that naturally boost your mood and help alleviate anxiety.

No one should face stress alone. A strong support network of family, friends, and professionals is essential in managing stress effectively. Family members can offer a listening ear and provide reassurance, while friends can share experiences and distractions that lighten the load. Professionals, such as therapists, counselors, or even trusted teachers, can offer guidance tailored to individual needs. Building a circle of support means knowing who to turn to when stress becomes overwhelming. The focus is creating a community that understands and uplifts, providing a sense of belonging and security.

The structure of daily life can also have a profound impact on stress levels. For many teens with autism, routines provide a sense of predictability and control, reducing anxiety. Having a consistent routine helps you know what to expect, minimizing the uncertainty that often leads to stress. Daily planners can be invaluable tools in creating and maintaining these routines. They allow you to organize tasks, set priorities, and allocate time for relaxation and hobbies. Visual schedules, with their clear and straightforward layouts, offer an easy way to keep track of activities and appointments. They serve as a constant reminder of what comes next, providing comfort through familiarity. It doesn't have to be a physical planner. I recently started using a shared family calendar app with my wife and college-age stepson to ensure we are all on the same page each week.

Incorporating these strategies into daily life requires patience and practice. From deep breathing to building a support network, each technique contributes to a comprehensive approach to stress management. Finding what works best for you might take some trial and error, and that's perfectly okay. You're not alone in this process. With the proper support and strategies, managing stress and anxiety becomes not just possible but a daily reminder of what you are capable of achieving.

BUILDING RESILIENCE: OVERCOMING CHALLENGES WITH CONFIDENCE

Resilience is like a rubber band. It stretches and bends but doesn't break. It's the ability to bounce back from setbacks and adapt to change. For teens on the spectrum, resilience is not just about surviving life's challenges but also about flourishing in the face of them. Life can throw curveballs—unexpected situations that test your limits. Resilience is crucial because it helps you navigate these twists and turns with confidence and poise. It develops personal growth, encouraging you to learn from experiences and emerge stronger.

Building resilience starts with setting realistic goals. Imagine setting out on a hike up a mountain. If your goal is to reach the summit in record time without preparation, you might find yourself struggling. Instead, break it down. Aim to reach the first scenic overlook, then the next, celebrating each milestone. This approach makes the journey manageable and motivates you to keep going. Similarly, setting achievable goals in daily life enables you to tackle challenges one step at a time, boosting your confidence with every success.

Positive self-talk is another powerful instrument for resilience. Picture the voice inside your head as your personal cheerleader. Instead of criticizing, it encourages and uplifts. When you encounter difficulties, remind yourself of your strengths and past achievements. Affirmations like "I can handle this" or "Every step counts" can shift your mindset from doubt to determination. This practice reinforces a positive outlook, transforming obstacles into opportunities for growth.

Setbacks are inevitable. They are part of life. However, rather than seeing them as failures, view them as learning experiences. When a project doesn't go as planned, take a moment to analyze what happened. Ask yourself what you can learn and how to improve next time. This reflective approach turns setbacks into stepping stones, each one contributing to your development. Remember, even the most successful individuals face setbacks. It's how you respond that defines your resilience.

Resilience often shines in everyday scenarios. Imagine facing a difficult social interaction. Maybe a conversation didn't go the way you hoped. Instead of dwelling on it, you reflect on what you could do differently next time. This adaptability helps you approach future interactions with confidence and grace. Academic challenges can test your resilience as well. Perhaps you struggled with a particular subject. Rather than giving up, you seek help, try new study techniques, and persist until you grasp the material. These instances of resilience are like hidden gems in daily life, each one strengthening your ability to overcome adversity.

Consider the story of Matt, a teen who faced challenges in mastering a musical instrument. Initially, the notes seemed jumbled, and frustration mounted. But Matt set small, achievable goals, focusing on one piece at a time. Encouraged by his progress, he practiced positive self-talk, reminding himself of his growing skills. Each setback —missed notes or tricky rhythms—became a lesson, not a failure. Over time, not only did Matt improve, but he also developed a resilient mindset that carried over into other areas of his life.

Building resilience is a process that requires effort and practice. Each experience, whether smooth or challenging, contributes to your growth. As you build resilience, you discover an inner strength that allows you to face life's challenges with confidence and courage.

NAVIGATING RELATIONSHIPS: FRIENDSHIPS AND SOCIAL DYNAMICS

As a teenager, relationships often feel like the heartbeat of your daily life, pulsing with excitement, confusion, and sometimes anxiety. For teens with autism, the social landscape comes with its own unique set of challenges and dynamics. Dealing with peer pressure can feel like walking a tightrope, balancing personal values against the desire to fit in with peers.

There's often a silent pressure to conform, whether it's about fashion choices, social media trends, or weekend plans. Understanding social hierarchies adds another layer to this complexity. In schools, these hierarchies can dictate who sits where at lunch or who gets invited to parties. Everyone seems to know they're like invisible rules, but no one really talks about them. For teens on the spectrum, decoding these unwritten rules can be overwhelming, leading to feelings of exclusion or misunderstanding.

Building healthy friendships is not just about finding someone to hang out with; it's about forming meaningful connections that enrich your life. It starts with identifying shared interests. Common interests provide a natural foundation for friendship, whether it's a love for video games, a passion for environmental issues, or a shared appreciation for a particular book series. These interests become the glue that holds friendships together, offering a comfortable space for connection and communication. Establishing boundaries is equally important. Healthy friendships require mutual respect and understanding of each other's limits. Communicating these boundaries clearly helps prevent misunderstandings and ensures that both friends feel valued and respected. Effective communication skills are at the heart of maintaining these relationships. Being able to express needs, listen actively, and resolve conflicts constructively are skills that strengthen bonds and create lifelong friendships.

Social interactions come with their own set of challenges, particularly for teens who might find interpreting social cues comparable to solving a complex math problem. Misinterpreting these cues, like facial expressions or tone of voice, can lead to awkward or uncomfortable situations. It's not uncommon for these misinterpretations to cause misunderstandings or conflicts. Coping with exclusion or bullying, unfortunately, is a reality for many teens. It's a painful experience that can deeply affect self-esteem and emotional well-being. Developing strategies to manage these situations, such as seeking support from trusted adults or engaging in activities that boost confidence, is crucial. Building resilience in the face of these challenges helps teens navigate social settings with greater assurance and self-worth.

A diverse social network offers many benefits beyond just having people to hang out with. Having a variety of friends and acquaintances introduces you to different perspectives, broadening your understanding and appreciation of the world. Each friend brings their own unique experiences and viewpoints, enriching conversations and offering new insights. This diversity enhances your social skills, allowing you to practice interacting with different personalities and adapting to various social contexts. Engaging with a wide range of individuals also fosters empathy and acceptance, teaching you to value diversity in all its forms.

For teens with autism, understanding and navigating social dynamics is a crucial part of personal growth. Building friendships based on mutual respect and shared interests while learning to manage social challenges equips teens with the skills they need to excel. As we explore these intricate relationships, we uncover the power of connection and the impact of empathy and understanding. Moving forward, we'll look at the world of practical life skills, exploring how to prepare for adulthood and independence.

3

SUPPORTING PARENTS ON THE JOURNEY

A family dinner is happening where everyone is chatting and sharing stories about their day. But not everyone at the table finds it easy to join in. This is a common scenario for families with a teenager on the spectrum, where communication can feel like a dance to a rhythm no one quite understands. It's a dance that requires patience, empathy, and creativity to master. You might wonder why your teen seems to misread the room or why a simple conversation can escalate into a misunderstanding. This chapter is dedicated to unraveling these mysteries and providing you with the devices to bridge the communication gap, creating stronger connections with your teen.

UNDERSTANDING YOUR TEEN'S WORLD: BRIDGING THE COMMUNICATION GAP

Communication challenges are often at the heart of misinterpretations between teens and their parents, especially among teens with autism. One of the most common barriers is the misinterpretation of nonverbal cues. Imagine trying to read a book where half the words are missing—this is often what social interactions feel like for teens on the spectrum. They might struggle to decipher facial expressions or body language, leading to confusion and frustration.

Additionally, differences in processing time can add another layer of complexity. While you might expect an immediate response to a question or comment, your teen might need a few extra moments to process the information and formulate a reply. This is not a sign of disinterest or defiance but rather a unique aspect of how their brain works.

Effective communication strategies are essential to overcome these challenges. Active listening exercises can be transformative. This involves not just hearing but truly listening—giving your full attention, acknowledging your teen's words, and reflecting back on what you've understood. This practice validates their feelings and creates a safe space for open dialogue. Visual aids can also enhance clarity, especially when discussing complex topics or plans. A simple chart or diagram can make abstract concepts more concrete, helping your teen grasp information more easily.

Patience and empathy are your greatest allies. Maintaining a calm demeanor during interactions can make a significant difference. When tensions rise, take a deep breath and remember that your teen is not intentionally challenging you; they are navigating a world that often feels overwhelming. Acknowledging their feelings is crucial even when you don't fully understand them. This validation shows that you respect their perspective and are willing to meet them halfway. The desire is to create an environment where they feel heard, respected, and understood.

Incorporating devices designed specifically for communication can also be invaluable. Communication apps tailored for autism offer innovative ways to express emotions and thoughts. These apps often include features like visual boards or speech-to-text options, making it easier for teens to articulate what they're feeling. Storytelling techniques can also be a powerful resource for expressing emotions. Encouraging your teen to share their experiences through written, spoken, or even drawn stories can help them explore and communicate their inner world.

CRAFTING A COMMUNICATION MAP

Consider creating a communication map with your teen. Start by identifying common topics or situations that lead to misunderstandings. Together, brainstorm visual or verbal cues that could help clarify these scenarios in the future. This collaborative exercise strengthens your communication skills and reinforces your partnership in confronting these challenges. Understanding and addressing these communication barriers opens the door to deeper connections and a more harmonious relationship with your teen. Communication is not just about exchanging words; it's about building a bridge to a world where both you and your teen feel understood and valued.

CREATING A SUPPORTIVE HOME ENVIRONMENT: PRACTICAL TIPS FOR DAILY LIFE

What happens if you are able to wake up each day knowing precisely what's coming next. For teens with autism, structure and routine can be like a comforting blanket, offering predictability in a world that often feels chaotic. Establishing a consistent routine at home is crucial for managing daily tasks and providing a sense of security. Visual schedules can be a game changer. Picture a simple chart that outlines the day's activities, from breakfast to bedtime, complete with pictures or symbols if words become overwhelming. These schedules help teens anticipate what's next and allow them to take ownership of their day. Designated quiet spaces are equally important. Think of them as personal retreats where your teen can escape the sensory overload of the world, even if just for a few minutes. These areas should be comfortable, perhaps with soft pillows or calming colors, offering a sanctuary where they can recharge.

The home environment itself can play a significant role in your teen's well-being. Sensory-friendly adaptations can make the difference between a house that feels like a battleground and one that feels like a haven. Consider the lighting first. Harsh, bright lights can be uncomfortable. Instead, opt for soft lighting options —think dimmer switches or lamps with warm bulbs. These create a more soothing atmosphere. Noise can also be an issue. Noise-reduction strategies, such as adding rugs or curtains, can help absorb sound and reduce echoes, making the environment less overwhelming. Even small changes like these can dramatically enhance comfort, promoting a sense of peace and safety.

Motivation and positive reinforcement can spark joy and accomplishment in this structured environment. Every teen, with autism or not, is looking for encouragement, whether or not they will admit it. Reward systems tailored to your teen's preferences can inspire them to reach goals. It could be earning extra screen time for completing chores or receiving a favorite treat after finishing homework.

These rewards don't just motivate; they celebrate achievements, no matter how small. Setting achievable goals is another way to boost confidence. Start with simple tasks, like organizing their study area, and gradually increase complexity as they succeed. Celebrating these successes creates a sense of capability and pride, reinforcing positive behaviors.

Even with the best efforts in place, conflicts pop up in even the most harmonious households. That's all part of people living together. How you manage these conflicts can significantly impact your teen's development. De-escalation strategies can be invaluable. When tempers flare, taking a moment to breathe deeply or stepping away for a short break can prevent arguments from escalating. Family meetings provide a platform for open discussions where everyone can voice concerns and explore solutions together. These meetings create opportunities for mutual understanding, teaching teens that conflicts can be resolved constructively. The ultimate goal is to build a home environment that supports their unique needs and nurtures their growth and resilience as they process the complexities of adolescence.

ENCOURAGING INDEPENDENCE: BALANCING SUPPORT WITH FREEDOM

As parents, it's natural to want to protect your children from the world's challenges. However, encouraging independence is crucial for personal growth, especially for teens with autism. Developing autonomy helps build confidence, allowing them to handle life with assurance. Think of decision-making as a muscle that strengthens with use. Each choice—whether choosing an outfit for the day or deciding on a weekend activity—contributes to a sense of self-efficacy. These seemingly small decisions accumulate, equipping teens with the skills to tackle more significant issues independently. Parental satisfaction comes from creating opportunities for them to explore their preferences and make informed choices, reinforcing their ability to manage their lives.

One practical way to encourage independence is by teaching essential life skills. Begin with something as fundamental as cooking simple meals. This skill not only promotes self-sufficiency but also boosts confidence. Start with basic recipes, like scrambled eggs or a simple pasta dish, gradually adding complexity as skills grow. Cooking can be a fun family activity, blending learning with bonding time. Likewise, managing personal finances is another crucial skill. Introduce concepts like budgeting and saving early on. You might start with a small allowance, encouraging your teen to track expenses and save for desired items. This practice instills a sense of responsibility and financial literacy, preparing them for the future.

Balancing support with autonomy is a delicate dance. On the one hand, you want to provide enough guidance to ensure safety and success. On the other hand, it's essential to allow room for exploration and mistakes. Gradually increasing responsibilities can help achieve this balance. For instance, start by assigning simple household tasks, then slowly increase their complexity as your teen demonstrates readiness. This gradual shift encourages growth without overwhelming them. Providing choices and options is another effective strategy. Instead of dictating every aspect of their day, offer options within set boundaries. This approach respects their autonomy while ensuring decisions remain manageable and safe.

In encouraging independence, remember that each teen's path will be unique. What works for one might not suit another. The key is to remain flexible, adjusting support as needed while celebrating every step towards autonomy. It's about enabling them to take charge of their lives, equipping them with the skills and confidence to explore the world on their own terms. By helping to give them independence, you're not just preparing them for adulthood but also enhancing their sense of self-worth and capability, laying the foundation for a fulfilling life.

HANDLING TRANSITIONS: SCHOOL CHANGES AND ROUTINE ADJUSTMENTS

Picture this: the school bell rings, signaling the end of class. The hallways fill with students rushing to their next destination. For many teens on the spectrum, this seemingly ordinary transition can spark anxiety. Transitions can feel like stepping into a whirlwind, disrupting the familiar routines that provide comfort and predictability. Change, whether moving to a new school year, adjusting to a different teacher, or even changing the daily schedule, can be a source of significant stress. The unfamiliarity of new environments or routines often leads to heightened anxiety as the brain works overtime to process the multitude of changes. This response is not unique; it's a common experience for many teens with autism who work best when there is consistency and predictability.

Preparation is key to helping handle these transitions more smoothly. You wouldn't start a trip or vacation without a map (well, without the GPS on your phone, at least). You would be setting yourself up to get lost and waste a lot of time. Similarly, preparing for change can ease the transition process. Creating a plan that outlines what to expect can be incredibly helpful. This might include visiting the new environment beforehand, such as a school open house or a meeting with the new teacher, to familiarize your teen with what's to come. Visual timelines can also provide a concrete representation of upcoming changes. By visually mapping out the steps involved in a transition, teens can see the progression and what to anticipate, reducing the uncertainty that often accompanies change.

These steps offer a sense of control and reassurance, making the abstract concept of change tangible and manageable.

Gradual adjustments act like a gentle slope instead of a steep hill, making transitions less abrupt and easier to handle. Incremental changes allow teens to acclimate at their own pace, minimizing the shock that comes with sudden shifts. For example, if a new school year is approaching, start by gradually adjusting sleep schedules weeks in advance to align with the new routine. Introduce new elements one at a time, such as practicing the route to school or adjusting meal times so that the new routine feels familiar by the time the change occurs. This approach respects the unique pace at which teens with autism adapt, providing the necessary time and space to adjust without feeling overwhelmed.

Working closely with educators is important in supporting transitions. Teachers are essential in creating a supportive environment that facilitates smooth changes. By working together, parents and educators can develop coordinated transition plans tailored to the teen's specific needs. Regular communication with school staff ensures everyone is on the same page, allowing for adjustments as needed. These plans might include strategies for easing into new classroom settings or incorporating sensory breaks throughout the day to help manage anxiety. Teachers who understand the nuances of each student's needs can provide targeted support, reinforcing the strategies implemented at home.

In negotiating transitions, it's vital to recognize the strength and resilience that teens on the spectrum demonstrate. These moments of change offer opportunities for growth and development, allowing teens to build adaptability and confidence. Transitions can become less frightening and more rewarding with the right support, preparation, and gradual adjustments.

ADVOCATING IN THE EDUCATIONAL SYSTEM: WORKING WITH SCHOOLS

You walk into a school meeting, the air thick with anticipation. You know that your child's educational future hinges on the discussions that unfold in these rooms. Advocacy in education is not just a buzzword—it's a lifeline. As a parent, your role in advocating for your teen's educational needs is crucial. You are their voice, their champion, ensuring that their unique needs are met within the educational system. Understanding educational rights is the first step in this journey. These rights are designed to protect your child and ensure they receive the support they deserve. Familiarize yourself with these rights; they are your foundation for building a case for your child's needs.

Effective advocacy requires a strategic approach, much like preparing for a chess match. Preparation is key before attending meetings with educators. Gather all necessary documentation, including your child's Individualized Education Program (IEP) and any relevant assessments or reports. This documentation serves as evidence, a tangible record of your child's progress and needs. Additionally, documenting communication and progress is vital. Keep records of emails, phone calls, and meetings with school staff. These records provide a paper trail, supporting your advocacy efforts and ensuring accountability from the school. They can also serve as a reference when you need to revisit discussions or address concerns.

Building a collaborative relationship with educators should be the primary objective. Think of it as forming a team where everyone works towards the same goal: your child's success. Regular updates and feedback loops are invaluable. Schedule consistent check-ins with teachers and school staff to discuss your child's progress and any areas of concern. These updates ensure that you are informed and involved in your child's education, allowing for adjustments as needed. Collaborative goal-setting is another critical aspect. Work with educators to set realistic, achievable goals for your child. These goals should be specific, measurable, and aligned with your child's abilities and aspirations. By setting these goals together, you will build a sense of partnership and shared responsibility.

Advocacy in education is a process that requires dedication and resilience. It's about standing firm in the belief that your child deserves the best possible support and opportunities. By understanding educational rights, preparing meticulously, and creating cooperative relationships with educators, you can effectively advocate for your teen's needs. You are not alone in this process. Resources and communities are ready to support you, providing guidance and encouragement along the way. As you muddle through the educational system, remember that your efforts will make a significant difference in your child's life, paving the way for a brighter, more inclusive future.

BUILDING A COMMUNITY: FINDING SUPPORT NETWORKS AND RESOURCES

Imagine standing in a room filled with others who share your experiences, laughing at jokes only you all understand. This is the power of community support for parents of teens with autism, where shared experiences and advice become lifelines. Connecting with other parents and professionals opens up a world of understanding and validation. In these spaces, you can exchange stories, learn new strategies, and find comfort in the knowledge that you're not alone on this path. Emotional support networks provide a safe haven where you can express frustrations without judgment and celebrate victories with those who truly get it.

Finding and accessing community resources can be a game changer. Local support groups are often the first step. These groups offer regular meetings where you can connect with others in your area, creating a sense of belonging and shared purpose. Online forums and communities expand this network globally, allowing you to engage with people from different backgrounds and perspectives. These digital spaces offer flexibility, letting you access support at any time, day or night. Such platforms can be an incredible source of information, from practical advice on daily challenges to the latest research in autism support.

Participating in autism-related events is another way to build and strengthen your community connections. Autism awareness workshops offer insights into the latest developments in understanding autism, often featuring experts who can provide valuable knowledge and resources. These events also create opportunities to meet other parents and professionals, broadening your support network. Family-friendly events and gatherings bring a sense of normalcy and joy, allowing your family to engage in fun activities without the pressure of judgment. These events celebrate diversity and inclusion, reinforcing the understanding that everyone deserves a place to belong.

Professional support plays a vital role in traversing the complexities of raising a teen with autism. Consulting with therapists and counselors provides expert guidance crafted to your family's unique needs. These professionals offer strategies to address specific challenges, such as managing anxiety or developing communication skills. They can also connect you with additional resources and services, expanding your support network even further. Accessing professional support is not a sign of weakness; it's a proactive step toward ensuring the best possible outcomes for your teen and your family.

BUILDING YOUR SUPPORT NETWORK

- **Local Support Groups:** Check with your community centers or local autism organizations for group meetings.
- **Online Forums:** Join forums like Autism Speaks or Wrong Planet to connect with a wider community.
- **Autism Awareness Workshops:** Look for events hosted by schools or autism advocacy groups.
- **Professional Support:** Consider therapists or counselors specializing in autism for tailored advice.

As you build your community, just keep in mind that every connection strengthens your support system. These networks not only provide practical assistance but also create spaces where you and your teen can prosper. With the right resources and support, handling the challenges of autism becomes a shared endeavor, filled with understanding, growth, and hope.

4

EDUCATOR STRATEGIES FOR INCLUSIVE CLASSROOMS

Picture a classroom where each student's eyes light up, not just because they've solved a tricky math problem but because they see their interests reflected in the lesson plan.

Envision a place where students with autism not only learn but excel, their unique strengths celebrated and leveraged. This is the vision for inclusive education, where adaptability and understanding create a space for every student to flourish. As educators, you hold the keys to unlocking this potential, crafting environments that not only accommodate but inspire.

INCLUSIVE TEACHING: CRAFTING AN AUTISM-FRIENDLY CURRICULUM

Designing a flexible curriculum that accommodates diverse learning needs is similar to creating a symphony with each student as an instrumentalist playing their instrument. Differentiated instruction techniques are the conductor's baton, guiding the class in harmony. This approach involves adapting lessons to meet the varied learning styles present in your classroom. For instance, when exploring a new science topic, offer students the choice to learn through reading, watching a video, or engaging in a hands-on experiment. By offering multiple pathways to understanding, you cater to auditory, visual, and kinesthetic learners, ensuring that no student is left behind.

Multi-sensory learning activities bring the lesson to life, engaging students through a combination of sight, sound, and touch. Consider teaching a history lesson not just through a textbook but by recreating a historical scene in the classroom. Students could dress up in period costumes, listen to music from that era, and even taste a dish from that time. These immersive experiences provide a richer understanding, particularly for students with autism who benefit from concrete and tangible learning opportunities.

Incorporating the interests and strengths of students on the spectrum is like adding a personal touch to a masterpiece. Leveraging student passions can significantly enhance engagement and motivation. If a student loves dinosaurs, why not integrate paleontology into a biology lesson?

Thematic projects based on these personal interests can transform education from mundane to magical, encouraging students to dive deeper into subjects they love while meeting curriculum standards. This approach boosts engagement and builds confidence, as students are more likely to succeed when working within their comfort zones.

Reducing sensory overload in learning materials is crucial for maintaining focus and comfort. Simplified presentation slides with clear fonts and muted colors can minimize distractions, allowing students to concentrate on the content. Ideally, you would have a classroom where the walls aren't cluttered with posters vying for attention but are instead thoughtfully arranged to promote calm and focus. This intentional design brings a serene learning environment where students with sensory sensitivities can perform at their best.

Including social-emotional learning components in your curriculum is important for developing well-rounded individuals. Role-playing exercises allow students to practice with social situations in a safe and controlled environment, building confidence and empathy. Picture a group of students working together to solve a mystery, each taking on a character with specific traits and challenges. This exercise enhances problem-solving skills and encourages understanding and acceptance of diverse perspectives.

Group collaboration activities provide opportunities for students to work together, improving teamwork and communication skills for teens on the spectrum and neurotypical students alike. When students collaborate on a project, they learn to appreciate each other's strengths and develop a sense of belonging. Whether it's creating a class mural or performing a play, these activities teach students the value of cooperation and the joy of shared success.

Remember that flexibility and creativity are your strongest allies in crafting an inclusive curriculum. By embracing each student's unique qualities and adapting your approach to meet their needs, you create a classroom where every student can shine. Your efforts enhance academic achievement and nurture a community of learners who respect and support one another.

VISUAL AIDS AND BEYOND: ENHANCING LEARNING FOR STUDENTS WITH AUTISM

It's the beginning of a new school year, and each student steps into a classroom where information dances across the walls, each visual element a stepping stone to understanding. Visual aids aren't just helpful—they're bridges to comprehension, especially for students on the spectrum who often work best with visual stimuli. Graphic organizers, for instance, serve as aids for the mind. They break down complex information into bite-sized, digestible pieces. These will allow students to see connections, whether they're mapping out historical events or plotting a story arc. Visual schedules, on the other hand, provide a comforting structure. They outline the day's activities, helping students antici-pate what's next and reducing anxiety about transitions. A simple chart displaying the day's agenda can be amazing, transforming chaos into clarity.

Technology brings an added dimension to visual learning, offering dynamic, interactive experiences. Educational apps designed for autism cater specifically to the learning styles of students on the spectrum, providing engaging content that adapts to their pace. These apps often include features like visual cues and interactive tasks that reinforce learning objectives. Interactive whiteboards are another powerful tool, turning static lessons into lively discussions. You can create a math problem to be solved in real time, with students actively participating and manipulating elements on the board. This hands-on approach enhances understanding and keeps students engaged and motivated.

When used thoughtfully, technology can transform the learning environment into a vibrant, interactive space.

Creating a visually structured classroom environment is similar to designing a sanctuary of learning. Clearly labeled stations guide students through activities, ensuring that they know exactly where to find what they need. This organization reduces confusion and enables independence as students navigate their learning environment. Color-coded materials further enhance this structure, providing visual cues that help students categorize and organize information. In this classroom, each subject could have its own color palette: math in blue, science in green, and literature in red. This system not only aids in organization but also supports memory retention as students begin to associate colors with specific subjects or tasks.

Visual storytelling and expression offer students a unique outlet for communication, tapping into their creativity and imagination. Storyboards for narrative writing, for example, allow students to plot their ideas visually before putting pen to paper. This method helps them organize their thoughts and see the story unfold, making the writing process less challenging. Art projects, too, provide a canvas for exploring themes and emotions. Whether it's a mural depicting a historical event or a collage representing personal experiences, visual arts enable students to express themselves in ways words sometimes cannot. These activities encourage self-expression and create a deeper connection to the material, making learning both personal and meaningful.

CREATE YOUR OWN STORYBOARD

Take a moment to think about a story you want to tell. It could be an adventure you've imagined or a real-life event. Use a storyboard template to sketch out the main scenes. Focus on the sequence of events and the key elements of your story. This exercise will help you visualize your narrative and organize your thoughts before writing. It's a fun and creative way to plan your story and explore different aspects of storytelling. By incorporating visual elements into your lesson plans, you not only cater to the needs of students with autism but also enrich the learning experience for the entire class. Visual aids, technology, and creative expression work together to create an inclusive environment where every student can succeed.

CLASSROOM DYNAMICS: PROMOTING EMPATHY AMONG PEERS

Every classroom should have an environment where every student feels like they belong, where the warmth of acceptance fills the room, and everyone is valued for who they are. Creating an inclusive classroom culture is about promoting this sense of belonging. It begins with activities that invite students to share their thoughts and listen to others. Circle-time discussions are a wonderful way to achieve this. Picture students gathered in a circle, each taking turns to share something about themselves—be it a weekend adventure or a favorite hobby. These discussions not only build communication skills but also allow students to appreciate each other's unique perspectives and experiences.

Team-building exercises further strengthen these bonds. Think of activities like trust falls or group problem-solving tasks. These exercises require cooperation and communication, helping students learn to rely on one another. They build camaraderie and teach the importance of working together, creating an environment where empathy and support are the norm. In such a setting, students are more likely to understand and accept their peers' differences, including those on the autism spectrum.

Implementing peer mentoring programs is another powerful strategy for nurturing supportive relationships. By pairing students together in peer buddy systems, you create opportunities for mentorship and friendship. Imagine an older student guiding a younger one through the school day, offering advice and companionship. This relationship benefits both parties: the mentor gains leadership skills, while the mentee receives guidance and support. For students on the spectrum, having a peer buddy can make handling social situations less intimidating, providing a familiar face in new or challenging environments.

Education about autism and neurodiversity is crucial for advancing understanding and acceptance. Providing materials and activities that teach students about these topics is a good place to start. Guest speakers on neurodiversity can offer firsthand insights, sharing personal stories that highlight the richness and diversity within the autism community. These talks can be eye-opening for students, breaking down stereotypes and misconceptions. Classroom workshops on empathy complement these lessons, encouraging students to put themselves in others' shoes and consider different perspectives. Through role-playing and interactive discussions, students learn the value of empathy, compassion, and respect.

I realize that we've touched on empathy a couple separate times now. That is how important empathy is at all levels (teens on the spectrum who don't know how to properly show it, parents helping them develop ways to improve it, and educators teaching it to neurotypical students).

Group projects that emphasize collaboration are the final step. Designing assignments that require cooperation and mutual respect teaches students to value each other's contributions. Group presentations, for instance, allow students to showcase their collective knowledge while learning from one another's strengths. Collaborative art projects offer a creative outlet for expression, where students can work together to create something beautiful. These projects encourage communication and compromise, vital skills for successful teamwork.

RANDOM ACTS OF KINDNESS

Consider creating a classroom challenge where students are encouraged to perform random acts of kindness for their peers. This could be as simple as holding the door open, sharing a snack, or offering a kind word. Have students reflect on how these acts made them feel and discuss the impact of kindness on building a supportive classroom environment. This exercise helps reinforce the importance of empathy and compassion in everyday interactions.

Promoting empathy among peers is not just shaping a classroom; it's cultivating a community where differences are celebrated and everyone feels valued. This environment enhances academic success and nurtures emotional growth, preparing students for a future where understanding and acceptance are commonplace.

MANAGING BEHAVIORAL CHALLENGES: PROACTIVE AND REACTIVE STRATEGIES

Visualize a classroom, a sanctuary for learning and discovery, suddenly buzzing with tension. A student is visibly distressed, and you wonder what triggered this response. Identifying the triggers and early warning signs of behavioral issues in students with autism is crucial.

Environmental stressors, like loud noises or bright lights, are common reasons. Consider the subtle hum of fluorescent lights or the chatter from a crowded hallway. For some students, these can feel overwhelming and persistent, like a swarm of bees. Changes in routine can also be unsettling for these teens. A substitute teacher or a last-minute schedule shift might seem minor, but for students on the spectrum, it can feel like the ground shifting beneath their feet. Recognizing these triggers early allows you to intervene before behavior escalates, creating a more harmonious classroom environment.

Developing proactive strategies to prevent behavioral challenges involves setting the stage for success. Consistent daily routines provide a sense of stability. When students know what to expect, anxiety decreases, and focus improves. Predictable classroom transitions are another cornerstone. Visual cues, such as a timer or a countdown, can help students mentally prepare for a shift in activities. By consistently signaling transitions, you reduce uncertainty and allow students to adjust smoothly. This approach minimizes the occurrence of disruptive behaviors, leading to a more peaceful and productive classroom.

Despite the best-laid plans, incidents do occur, and having reactive strategies in place is crucial. Calm-down corners serve as safe spaces where students can retreat to regain composure. Picture a cozy nook with soft pillows and sensory tools, offering solace and a moment of respite. These corners encourage self-regulation, allowing students to process their emotions without judgment. De-escalation techniques also play a vital role. Speaking in a calm, steady voice and offering choices can help defuse tension and redirect focus. Gentle reminders and positive reinforcement guide students back to a state of equilibrium, reducing the impact of behavioral incidents on the classroom dynamic.

Collaboration with support staff is the backbone of effective behavior management. By working with aides and specialists, you create a network of support tailored to each student's needs. Behavior intervention plans (BIPs) are at the heart of this collaboration. These plans outline specific strategies and interventions, ensuring consistency across different settings. Regular team meetings provide opportunities to review progress, share insights, and adjust approaches as needed. This cooperative effort encourages a unified approach, reinforcing positive behaviors and addressing challenges comprehensively.

Understanding and managing behavioral challenges in the classroom requires patience and a strategic approach. By identifying triggers, implementing proactive and reactive strategies, and collaborating with support staff, you create an environment where students with autism can accomplish anything. This holistic approach not only supports individual growth but also enriches the entire classroom community.

COLLABORATION WITH PARENTS: BUILDING PARTNERSHIPS FOR SUCCESS

Envision a world where the classroom isn't a separate universe from home but rather an extension of it. This seamless connection starts with establishing open lines of communication between teachers and parents. We aren't talking about the occasional report card or a hurried conversation at school events. Regular and transparent communication is key to building trust and understanding. Weekly progress updates can serve as a consistent touchpoint, informing parents about their child's achievements and challenges. These updates don't need to be extensive—just a snapshot of the week can make a world of difference.

On the other hand, parent-teacher conferences offer a more in-depth opportunity to discuss the student's progress. These meetings should be a dialogue where insights are shared and strategies are developed together. When parents and teachers work together, students feel supported, knowing that the adults in their lives are united in their efforts.

Aligning on educational goals and strategies ensures consistency between the classroom and home. Joint goal-setting sessions invite parents to participate in the educational planning process, combining the best of classroom strategies with home support.

Whether it's reinforcing a particular skill or celebrating a new milestone, these sessions create a unified approach to learning. Sharing resources and materials further bridges the gap, providing parents with the tools they need to support their child's education at home. Imagine sending home a packet with simple activities or tips that complement classroom lessons. This partnership not only enhances the student's learning experience but also allows parents to take a more active role in their child's education.

Parents are the ultimate source of information when it comes to their children. Seeking parental input and insights is invaluable. Parent questionnaires can be a simple yet effective way to gather this information. These questionnaires might ask about the child's interests, preferred learning styles, or any particular challenges they face. By understanding these nuances, educators can modify their approach, creating a learning environment that resonates with each student. This practice acknowledges that parents know their children best and honors their role as equal participants in the educational process.

Creating a supportive network for parents involves more than just inviting them to school events. Parent volunteer opportunities allow parents to engage directly with the school, whether helping out during class activities, organizing events, or assisting with field trips. These opportunities bring a sense of belonging and investment in the school community. Family-inclusive events, such as potlucks or open classroom days, provide a relaxed setting for families to interact with one another and with educators. These gatherings build relationships, strengthen community bonds, and create a supportive network where everyone feels welcome and valued.

Building these partnerships requires effort and commitment from both educators and parents. When that happens, doors will open that invite cooperation and nurturing relationships that benefit the student. When schools and families work together, the result is a richer, more supportive educational experience for teens with autism.

CONTINUOUS LEARNING: PROFESSIONAL DEVELOPMENT IN AUTISM EDUCATION

Visualize a classroom where every educator is equipped with the latest knowledge and strategies to support students on the spectrum. This isn't just a dream—it's an achievable goal through ongoing professional development. Continuous learning is the lifeline that keeps teaching practices fresh and effective. Attending autism workshops and seminars provides educators with the latest insights and practical tools. These sessions often feature experts in the field who share cutting-edge research and innovative approaches. They're like a refreshing splash of inspiration that reinvigorates teaching methods and broadens understanding. Online courses and certifications offer another avenue for growth. These flexible learning options allow educators to deepen their expertise at their own pace, making professional development accessible and convenient. The more you learn, the better equipped you are to meet your students' diverse needs, creating an environment where every student can succeed.

Partnerships among educators are another powerful vehicle for growth. Peer learning turns teaching into a shared adventure where experiences and insights are exchanged openly. Teacher mentoring programs pair seasoned educators with newcomers, creating a fresh exchange of ideas and strategies. This mentorship not only supports new teachers but also enriches the knowledge of veteran educators, who gain new perspectives from their mentees. Collaborative lesson planning is another effective strategy. When teachers come together to design lessons, they pool their creativity and expertise, crafting more engaging and inclusive curriculums. This collective effort results in a richer learning experience for students and a more supportive professional environment for educators.

Staying updated on autism research is crucial for maintaining effective teaching practices. Educational journals are full of knowledge, offering in-depth articles and studies that explore various aspects of autism education. Subscribing to these journals keeps you informed about the latest findings and trends, allowing you to integrate evidence-based practices into your teaching. Autism-focused webinars can provide another valuable resource. These online sessions often feature leading researchers and practitioners discussing emerging topics and sharing practical strategies. They offer a convenient way to access expert knowledge from the comfort of your own home or classroom. By staying informed, you ensure that your teaching methods remain relevant and effective, ultimately benefiting your students.

Reflective practice is the secret ingredient in continuously improving your teaching. This requires taking a step back to evaluate your methods and identify areas for growth. Reflective journals are an excellent tool for this purpose. By regularly documenting your experiences and reflections, you gain insights into what works and what doesn't, allowing you to make informed adjustments. Peer feedback sessions offer another layer of reflection. Inviting colleagues to observe your teaching and provide constructive feedback gives you valuable perspectives that can enhance your practice. This openness to feedback creates a culture of continuous improvement, where educators support one another in their professional growth. Reflective practice is all about seeking opportunities to refine and enhance your teaching, ensuring that you provide the best possible support for your students.

You create a dynamic and responsive teaching environment by embracing continuous learning, collaboration, and reflection. This commitment to growth enhances your professional skills and enriches the educational experience for all of your students, both on the spectrum and neurotypical alike. As you continue to evolve as an educator, you lay the groundwork for a classroom that is inclusive, engaging, and responsive to the needs of all learners.

5

SOCIAL SKILLS AND PEER INTERACTIONS

Y ou have just stepped into a room where everyone seems to be speaking a secret language—one that's communicated not through words but through subtle gestures, fleeting glances, and expressive faces. For many teens with autism, this is the reality they face in social settings, where non-verbal communication plays a crucial role. Understanding these cues is like having a key to unlock the mysteries of social interactions, allowing you to connect more deeply with others. Non-verbal communication includes everything from body language to facial expressions, and it speaks volumes even when no words are exchanged. It's the unspoken dialogue that accompanies conversation, often setting the tone and conveying emotions more vividly than words ever could.

Take body language, for instance. A simple nod can signal agreement, while crossed arms might suggest defensiveness or discomfort. Learning to interpret these signals can transform social interactions, helping you respond appropriately to the unspoken messages others send. Facial expressions are equally telling. A smile can convey warmth and friendliness, while a furrowed brow might indicate confusion or concern.

Recognizing these expressions allows you to gauge the emotions of those around you. By sharpening these skills, you can navigate social landscapes with greater ease and confidence, strengthening your connections with peers.

But how do you go about decoding these non-verbal signals? The best place to begin is with practice. Start with eye contact, a foundational element of non-verbal communication. Eye contact is like the handshake of the eyes, establishing a connection and showing attentiveness. Practice making eye contact in comfortable settings, gradually increasing the duration as it feels more natural. Observing body posture is another valuable technique. Notice how people stand or sit in different situations, whether they're relaxed, tense, or open. This awareness will help you interpret the context of interactions more accurately, improving your social intuition.

Interpreting social cues can be challenging, especially when gestures or expressions are misinterpreted. You might encounter situations where you assume someone is upset when they're simply deep in thought or miss a cue that indicates someone wants to change the topic. Overlooking subtle cues is a common hurdle, as these signals can be brief and difficult to notice. The important thing to remember is to approach these challenges with patience and a willingness to learn. Everyone makes mistakes in social interactions, and each experience is an opportunity to improve your skills.

Various resources are available to support your goal of mastering nonverbal communication. Social skills workshops offer structured environments where you can practice these skills with guidance and feedback. These workshops often include activities like interpreting facial expressions or role-playing scenarios, providing a safe space to explore and develop your abilities. Interactive online games can also be helpful, offering engaging ways to practice spotting social cues in a virtual setting. These games often simulate real-life situations, allowing you to experiment with different responses and observe their outcomes.

For those looking to enhance their nonverbal communication skills even further, consider adding tools and activities to their routine. Interactive apps designed to improve social skills can be a fun way to practice. These apps often include visual guides and quizzes that test your ability to recognize and respond to various nonverbal signals.

Additionally, joining a local club or group focused on social skills development can provide invaluable peer support and encouragement. By actively engaging in these activities, you can build your confidence and proficiency in interpreting non-verbal communication, leading to more meaningful and rewarding interactions with those around you.

NON-VERBAL COMMUNICATION JOURNAL

Keep a journal to document your observations of non-verbal communication in daily interactions. Note specific gestures, expressions, or postures you encounter and how they influence the conversation. Reflect on how accurately you interpreted these cues and consider what you might do differently next time. This exercise will help reinforce your learning and provide insights into your progress.

ROLE-PLAYING SCENARIOS: PRACTICING REAL-LIFE SITUATIONS

Consider walking onto a stage, not to perform in a grand theater, but to rehearse the everyday scenes of life. Role-playing offers a unique opportunity to practice social interactions in a controlled, supportive environment—think of it as a dress rehearsal for real-world encounters. For teens with autism, this can be incredibly helpful, allowing them to build social confidence and work on their skills without the pressure of immediate real-life consequences. By engaging in role-playing, teens can explore various scenarios, from introducing themselves to new people to having complex conversations. This creates a space where mistakes are not only accepted but valued as learning experiences, where each "scene" helps develop strategies for future interactions.

Setting up effective role-playing sessions requires a bit of planning to make sure they are productive and realistic. Start by defining clear objectives for each session. Are you focusing on initiating conversations or perhaps on resolving conflicts calmly? Knowing the goal helps steer the session to meet specific needs. Creating a safe and supportive environment is equally important. This means establishing ground rules that make it safe for participants to feel comfortable expressing themselves. Consider using familiar settings or props to make the scenarios more relatable, reducing anxiety and strengthening engagement. This approach helps teens immerse themselves in the role-playing experience, making it more meaningful and impactful.

Let's consider some specific scenarios that can be practiced through role-playing. Introducing oneself to new people is an everyday social interaction, yet it can be intimidating. Practicing this scenario allows teens to experiment with different ways of breaking the ice and finding what feels most comfortable for them. Another valuable scenario is initiating and maintaining conversations. This involves practicing how to start a dialogue, keep it flowing, and knowing when to wrap it up—all great skills for building and maintaining friendships. Finally, resolving conflicts calmly is a major skill that can be explored through role-playing. By simulating disagreements, teens can practice expressing their feelings assertively and finding common ground, creating healthier relationships.

Feedback and reflection are large factors in role-playing, transforming practice into growth. After each session, encourage feedback to provide different perspectives on the interactions. This feedback should be constructive, highlighting strengths and offering suggestions for improvement. Additionally, self-assessment checklists can be a powerful resource for personal reflection. These checklists allow teens to evaluate their performance, identify areas for growth, and set goals for future sessions. By engaging in both peer and self-reflection, teens can gain a deeper understanding of their social skills, reinforcing their learning and boosting their confidence.

Role-playing can help teens approach social situations with increased confidence and competence, knowing they've rehearsed and refined their skills. The lessons learned in these sessions extend beyond the confines of the role-playing environment, preparing teens to overcome the complexities of social interactions in their daily lives. This practice brings a sense of mastery over social challenges, paving the way for more authentic and fulfilling connections with others.

BUILDING CONFIDENCE: OVERCOMING SOCIAL ANXIETY

Social anxiety can feel like an unwelcome guest who shows up unannounced, often at the most inconvenient times. For teens with autism, it can be even more troublesome, with triggers like fear of judgment and unpredictable social settings lurking around every corner. Picture walking into a room where you're unsure of the rules, where the possibility of misunderstanding or being misunderstood hangs over you like a heavy cloud. This fear of judgment can make social interactions feel like walking a tightrope, where one wrong move risks exposure or embarrassment. First, there is worrying about what others might think. Then, there is the pressure of expectations, both real and imagined, that can weigh heavily on your shoulders. Unpredictable social settings, like a crowded cafeteria or a bustling school dance, can amplify these feelings, creating an environment where anxiety runs wild. The unpredictability of these situations—the uncertainty of who'll be there, what conversations will happen, or how to handle the various social situations—can be overwhelming.

Yet, there are ways to build social confidence, to step out of the shadows of anxiety and into the light of self-assurance. One powerful weapon is the use of positive affirmations. These are like little pep talks you give yourself, reminding you of your strengths and capabilities. By repeating affirmations like "I am capable," or "I can handle this," you begin to rewire your thinking, replacing doubt with confidence. These reminders will shift your mindset, focusing on your potential rather than your fears. Social skills coaching can also be incredibly rewarding. This involves working with someone who can guide you through the complexities of social interaction, offering strategies designed for your specific needs. You can learn techniques to handle conversations, interpret social cues, and build genuine connections through coaching. It's like having a personal guide to help you traverse the complex social landscape, offering support and encouragement along the way.

Another effective approach is gradual exposure, a technique that involves slowly increasing your exposure to social environments. Think of it like dipping your toes in the water before diving in. Start with smaller gatherings, where the stakes feel lower, and the setting is more intimate. These could be a lunch with a few friends or a small group activity. You can gradually participate in larger group activities as you gain comfort and confidence. The key is to pace yourself, taking one step at a time and celebrating each small victory. This gradual process allows you to build resilience and confidence, helping you feel more comfortable in social settings over time.

Many examples of success stories illustrate the transformative power of overcoming social anxiety. Consider Alex, a shy teen on the spectrum who, once hesitant to speak up, decided to join a school club. Initially, the idea of attending meetings filled him with dread, but over time, he found a sense of belonging and purpose. The club offered a structured environment where he could connect with other teens who shared similar interests, gradually building his confidence through shared activities and discussions. Another inspiring story involves Barb, a teen who began volunteering at local community events. Initially overwhelmed by the prospect of interacting with strangers, she discovered that volunteering provided a sense of structure and clarity. The assigned tasks offered a focus beyond social interaction, allowing her to engage more comfortably and genuinely with others.

Through these experiences, she not only developed confidence but also discovered a newfound passion for community service.

These stories remind us that social anxiety, while challenging, is not insurmountable. With the right strategies and support, teens with autism can learn to manage anxiety and build meaningful connections. The key is taking small, intentional steps, building confidence along the way, and discovering the joy of authentic interaction.

THE IMPORTANCE OF BOUNDARIES: ESTABLISHING HEALTHY RELATIONSHIPS

You wouldn't try to build a fort without walls—that would be impossible and not make sense. That's what life is like without personal boundaries. Boundaries are the invisible lines that define how we interact with others and the world. They're extremely important in respecting personal space and managing emotional exchanges. Personal space boundaries help you understand the comfortable distance to maintain between yourself and others, varying depending on the relationship. Emotional boundaries, on the other hand, protect your feelings and energy, making sure that you don't take on more than you can handle emotionally. Boundaries are the blueprint for healthy relationships, guiding interactions in a way that respects both parties involved. Misunderstandings and discomfort can happen without them, leading to strained connections.

Establishing and communicating boundaries is a skill that requires practice and patience. It often begins with understanding what feels comfortable for you and what doesn't. Assertive communication techniques can be invaluable here, allowing you to express your needs and limits clearly and respectfully. This means using "I" statements to convey your feelings without blaming others, such as "I feel overwhelmed when..." rather than "You're overwhelming me by...". This approach opens the door to constructive dialogue. Boundary-setting worksheets can also provide a structured way to identify and better express your boundaries, helping you to map out scenarios where you need to set limits and how you plan to communicate them. These devices not only clarify your own needs but also guide others in understanding how to interact with you in ways that feel safe and respectful.

Maintaining boundaries, however, is not without its challenges. You might encounter situations where your boundaries are tested or even violated, whether intentionally or unintentionally. Handling boundary violations requires courage and clarity. It is important to address these situations promptly and assertively, reminding others of your established limits while maintaining a respectful tone. Balancing empathy with self-care is another obstacle. You might feel like you should prioritize others' needs over your own, which can lead to burnout or resentment. Maintaining boundaries is not about being inflexible but rather ensuring your well-being while still showing compassion. It's perfectly okay to help others, but it's also crucial to recognize when doing so might compromise your own emotional health.

Boundaries play a significant role in promoting mutual respect and understanding in the context of relationships. They help build trust, as classmates and friends can rely on each other to respect their needs and limits. This trust forms the foundation for healthy, supportive relationships where both parties feel valued and understood. Encouraging open communication about boundaries further strengthens these connections, allowing for honest discussions about comfort levels and expectations. When boundaries are respected, it creates a safe space for individuals to express themselves genuinely, enhancing the depth and richness of the relationship.

Boundaries are not just about keeping people out; they're about defining how you let people in. They're the framework that supports strong, healthy relationships, allowing for growth and connection without losing oneself in the process. By respecting and defining these invisible lines, you allow yourself to engage with others in fulfilling and acceptable ways.

NAVIGATING BULLYING: STRATEGIES FOR PROTECTION AND RESOLUTION

After finishing your homework, you take a break and grab your phone. You open it up to check messages and suddenly see many hurtful comments lighting up the screen, each one more vicious than the last. This is cyberbullying in its rawest form, a shadowy presence that follows you even when you're physically alone. For teens with autism, who may already feel like outsiders in a world that doesn't always understand them, the impact of cyberbullying can be intense. It comes down to more than just hurt feelings. That would be bad enough. No, this is about the erosion of self-esteem and the constant reminder that someone is targeting you.

Cyberbullying, unlike traditional forms, doesn't have physical boundaries. It finds you at school, at home, and everywhere in between, making it relentless and pervasive. But it's not the only form of bullying. Verbal harassment, with its sharp words and derogatory names, cuts deep, leaving emotional scars that are invisible yet painfully real. Physical harassment, though less common, is equally damaging, creating an environment of fear and insecurity. Each form of bullying, whether digital or physical, chips away at the sense of safety and belonging that every teen deserves.

So, what can you do when faced with bullying? You need to take the following practical steps. First, reporting incidents to trusted adults is crucial. This might be a teacher, a parent, or a school counselor—anyone who can intervene and provide support. Don't hesitate to report bullying; keeping it secret only gives it more power. Developing a support network is another vital strategy. Surround yourself with friends who uplift you, family who will listen to you, and mentors who guide you. These relationships act as a buffer, providing emotional strength and reassurance. You're not alone, and there are people ready to stand by your side.

Resilience and self-advocacy play pivotal roles in combating bullying. Resilience is like a muscle that grows stronger each time you face adversity and choose to rise above it. Every time you bounce back, you show that you will not let the words or actions of others define your worth. Self-advocacy, on the other hand, empowers you to stand up assertively. It means using your voice to express your boundaries and demand respect. Practice saying, "I don't appreciate being spoken to that way," or "Please stop; this is not okay." Simple yet powerful statements reinforce your right to be treated with dignity.

There are numerous resources and support systems available for those dealing with bullying. Anti-bullying organizations provide helpful information, resources, and devices for prevention and intervention. They offer platforms where your voice can be heard, stories shared, and solutions found. School counseling services are another resource that shouldn't be overlooked. Counselors are trained to handle bullying situations and can offer guidance, mediation, and emotional support. They can help you create an action plan, making sure that you have the strategies that you will need to protect yourself and encourage resilience. These resources are not just lifelines; they're communities dedicated to creating safer environments for everyone.

In the end, handling bullying requires a combination of action, support, and inner strength. You must learn when to seek help, how to protect yourself, and understand that you have the right to live in spaces free from fear and intimidation. Bullying, in all its forms, is a challenge no one should face alone, and with the right tools and support, it's possible to rise above it and reclaim your sense of safety and self-worth. Remember, being bullied is never your fault, and seeking help is a courageous step toward healing and empowerment.

CELEBRATING DIVERSITY: EMBRACING DIFFERENCES IN SOCIAL CIRCLES

What would the world look like if painted in just one color? It might be striking initially, but the novelty would soon wear thin, leaving a landscape lacking depth and vibrancy. Social interactions are much the same; they improve with diversity, bringing together a spectrum of perspectives and experiences that better our understanding of the world. Embracing diversity is a large part of personal growth, particularly for teens with autism going through a world that often feels rigid and narrow. Interacting with people from different backgrounds exposes you to new ways of thinking. You learn to appreciate that there isn't just one way to view the world. Each person you meet offers a unique lens, broadening your horizons.

Friends from different cultures introduce you to new traditions, cuisines, and languages, sparking curiosity and appreciation for the vastness of human experience. These friendships challenge preconceived notions, encouraging you to question stereotypes and embrace inclusivity. The benefits extend beyond cultural awareness; diverse friendships improve adaptability and resilience, teaching you to handle different social norms and communication styles. You learn to find common ground amid differences, a skill that proves invaluable in all aspects of life.

Creating inclusive environments requires intention and effort. It starts with the language we use. Inclusive language acknowledges and respects differences, avoiding assumptions and stereotypes. Encouraging everyone to contribute their voice brings a sense of belonging, ensuring no one feels left out. This might mean tweaking activities to accommodate different needs or simply being open to new ideas and perspectives. In a classroom or community setting, encourage collaboration through projects that require input from all members. This approach enriches the final outcome and strengthens relationships, as each person feels valued for their unique contributions.

Celebrating diversity in social circles is about recognizing the richness that each individual brings to your life; it is not just about inclusion. This encourages you to step outside your bubble, to embrace the unfamiliar, and to learn from those around you. In doing so, you grow as an individual and a member of a broader, more interconnected community. This chapter has explored the complicated nature of social interactions, from understanding boundaries to handling bullying. As we move forward, we'll get into preparing for adulthood and independence and work on training you with the skills and confidence to excel in the world beyond high school.

6

PREPARING FOR ADULTHOOD
AND INDEPENDENCE

You are sitting at your kitchen table on a blustery Saturday morning in the fall. The aroma of fresh coffee fills the air, and the sizzle of bacon sounds like sweet, sweet music. This isn't just an everyday breakfast. No, this is a validation of the life skills that have equipped you for independent living. For teenagers with autism, the transition to adulthood is a significant milestone, requiring a knowledge of essential skills. These skills aren't just about surviving. They allow you to walk through life with confidence and self-reliance.

LIFE SKILLS 101: ESSENTIAL SKILLS FOR DAILY LIVING

At the core of independent living lies the mastery of life skills. Personal hygiene routines are a fundamental aspect of daily life, ensuring cleanliness, self-respect, and confidence. From brushing teeth to maintaining skincare routines, these practices become second nature with practice. Cooking basic meals is another important skill. You don't need to become a gourmet chef (unless you want to!). However, you do need to learn how to scramble eggs or boil pasta, along with a few other simple dishes. Who knows? You may want to have family or friends over for an evening dinner party. Home maintenance tasks round out this list of skills. Simple acts like changing a light bulb or unclogging a drain allow teens to take control of their environments, creating a sense of ownership and pride.

Teaching these skills effectively requires a structured approach. Step-by-step instructional guides serve as priceless resources, breaking down tasks into manageable pieces. Visual checklists are another powerful device, providing clear visual cues that guide teens through each task step. These checklists can be placed in strategic locations, like near the bathroom mirror or on the fridge, acting as gentle reminders of daily responsibilities. Practice and repetition are the keys to mastery. Consistent weekly skill-building sessions can transform these once-challenging tasks into routine activities.

Access to resources for skill development is essential. Online tutorials and videos offer accessible, engaging ways to learn new tasks, catering to different learning styles. Platforms like YouTube are filled with channels dedicated to teaching everything from cooking basics to home repair tips. Community workshops provide hands-on experience and interaction with instructors who can offer personalized guidance. These workshops can also be social opportunities, allowing teens to connect with peers who share similar goals.

Skill Development Devices

- **Online Tutorials:** Websites like YouTube and Skillshare offer free and paid courses on a variety of life skills.
- **Community Workshops:** Check local community centers or adult education programs for cooking or home maintenance workshops.
- **Visual Checklists:** Create personalized checklists using online templates to break down tasks into simple steps.

As teens develop these skills, they gain more than just the ability to perform tasks. They build confidence, independence, and a sense of accomplishment. Each skill learned is a step towards self-reliance, preparing them for the various responsibilities that come with adulthood. In this chapter, we'll explore the tools and strategies that empower teens to navigate life's challenges.

CAREER EXPLORATION: FINDING AND PURSUING INTERESTS

We've all seen movies or pictures of an individual standing at a crossroads, with each path leading to a different future. Deciding what you will do for a living is very much like this example. The choice can seem scary, but it's also an exciting opportunity to explore what truly sparks your interest. For teens with autism, discovering career interests begins with identifying passions that could translate into fulfilling careers. One effective method is using interest inventories. These tools, often in the form of quizzes or assessments, help pinpoint what excites you. They might reveal a hidden love for technology, a knack for creative writing, or a fascination with biology. The key is to keep an open mind and explore a wide range of possibilities.

Job shadowing experiences offer a valuable glimpse into potential career paths. Imagine spending a day with a software engineer, observing their daily tasks, and gaining insights into what the job entails. Such experiences provide a firsthand look at the working world, helping you understand the day-to-day responsibilities and skills required. They also allow you to ask questions and learn directly from professionals in the field. Whether it's a day at a veterinary clinic or a week at a graphic design studio, job shadowing can highlight paths you might not have considered before.

Internships and volunteer work are gateways to gaining real-world experience and building a resume. Local internship programs offer structured environments where you can apply and develop skills relevant to your chosen field. Internships might involve working with a company or organization, allowing you to contribute to projects and learn from mentors. Volunteer roles in community organizations also provide valuable experience, often with more flexibility. Whether it's helping at a local animal shelter, assisting in a library, or participating in environmental clean-ups, volunteering creates a sense of responsibility and teamwork. Both internships and volunteer work offer the chance to build a network of contacts that can be helpful in your future career.

Developing job-related skills is ideal as you pursue your interests. Enrolling in skill-specific courses can provide the technical knowledge needed for specific careers. Whether it's a coding boot camp for tech enthusiasts or a photography class for aspiring artists, these courses offer hands-on learning. Participating in vocational training programs can also be advantageous, especially for careers that require practical skills. These programs often include on-the-job training, helping you gain experience while learning. The combination of education and real-world practice equips you with the skills employers are looking for.

Networking within your chosen field is vital. Building professional connections opens doors to opportunities and provides guidance from those already established in the industry. Attending industry events like conferences or workshops allows you to meet professionals and learn about the latest trends and developments. These events also showcase your enthusiasm and interest, making a positive impression on potential employers. Joining professional organizations is another way to expand your network. These organizations often offer resources, mentorship programs, and networking events that can help you connect with like-minded individuals.

Career exploration is not just about finding a job; it's about finding a path that aligns with your passions and strengths. It's about discovering what excites you to get up each morning and enthusiastically pursue your goals. The journey to finding and pursuing your interests is filled with opportunities to learn, grow, and connect with others who share your passion. By taking advantage of these resources and experiences, you equip yourself with the tools to succeed in the career that truly fits you.

HIGHER EDUCATION: NAVIGATING COLLEGE AND VOCATIONAL PATHS

The world of higher education opens doors to a future filled with knowledge and growth, offering diverse paths tailored to individual strengths and aspirations. For many, the traditional route of a four-year university provides a broad education with opportunities to explore various subjects and develop skills in a chosen field. Universities often boast vibrant campus life, where learning extends beyond the classroom, nurturing personal development through clubs, sports, and social interactions. This environment can be ideal for those seeking a comprehensive academic experience and a rich social atmosphere.

However, not every teen finds their fit within the walls of a large university. Community colleges offer a valuable alternative, providing the first two years of undergraduate education at a more manageable scale and often a lower cost. These institutions allow students to explore different subjects before committing to a major, with the flexibility to transfer to a four-year college if desired. Community colleges also cater to diverse learning needs, offering smaller classes and more personalized attention, which can be particularly helpful for students with autism.

Vocational schools provide specialized training in fields such as culinary arts, automotive technology, or healthcare for those with a clear career focus. These programs are designed to equip students with practical skills that lead directly to employment, often including hands-on experience through internships or apprenticeships. Vocational education can be an excellent choice for teens eager to enter the workforce quickly with a set of marketable skills, bypassing the broader academic requirements of traditional colleges.

The path to higher education begins with the application process, a journey that can feel like running a marathon for both students and parents. Researching potential schools is the first step, considering factors such as location, size, programs offered, and campus culture. Once a shortlist of schools is identified, it's time to tackle the applications. Keeping track of deadlines is crucial, as missing a deadline can close the door on an opportunity. Writing personal statements is another important detail, and it's a chance for students to share their unique stories and perspectives. These essays should highlight strengths, passions, and how the student envisions their future, offering a glimpse into what they will bring to the campus community.

There is more to higher education than just about choosing the right school. It is also important to make sure the necessary support is in place to succeed. Many institutions offer accommodations and support services tailored to the needs of students on the spectrum. Disability services offices are a valuable resource, assisting with everything from note-taking services to exam accommodations. These offices work with students to develop individualized plans that address specific needs, ensuring equal access to educational opportunities. Academic tutoring programs offer additional support, helping students stay on track with coursework and develop effective study habits.

There are many various success stories of individuals with autism who have thrived in higher education, often by leveraging these resources. First, there's the story of Emma, a graduate who turned her love for technology into a successful career in software development. With the support of her university's disability services, she excelled in her studies, securing internships that paved the way for her career. Then there's Alex, who found his niche in a community college's culinary program, where the hands-on learning environment allowed him to exceed even his own expectations. With accommodations tailored to his learning style, Alex graduated with honors and now works as a chef in a renowned restaurant.

These stories validate the power of higher education in unlocking potential and pursuing passions. They highlight the importance of choosing paths that align with individual strengths and interests while ensuring that support systems are in place to improve success. Higher education should not be a one-size-fits-all endeavor. Personalizing it for each student gives everyone an equal opportunity to make the most of their experience.

FINANCIAL LITERACY: MANAGING MONEY AND BUDGETS

Understanding basic financial concepts can help you make financial decisions more straightforward, such as deciding if you can afford to buy that new tech gadget you saw on Amazon. Let's start with budgeting basics. A budget is like a roadmap for your money, showing where it comes from and where it goes. It helps you manage your income and expenses so you don't end up with too much month at the end of your money. By setting aside funds for essentials like food and rent and for fun activities, you ensure financial stability and peace of mind. Understanding credit and debt is also important. Credit allows you to borrow money for purchases, but it must be repaid with interest, which is the cost of borrowing. Managing debt responsibly means keeping track of what you owe and paying it back on time to avoid high-interest charges while maintaining a good credit score.

Managing your income and expenses effectively requires a practical approach. Start by creating a monthly budget. This involves listing all your sources of income, such as a part-time job or allowance, and all your expenses, including bills and leisure activities. By comparing these lists, you can determine if you're living within your means or if adjustments are necessary. Tracking expenses using apps can simplify this process, allowing you to categorize spending and identify patterns. These apps often send alerts when you approach your budget limits, helping you stay on track. Financial discipline is about making informed choices, like skipping a daily coffee run to save for a bigger goal, such as a new car or a holiday trip.

Saving and investing are core components of financial well-being. Saving money means putting aside some of your income for future needs or emergencies. Opening a savings account is a safe way to store money while earning a small amount of interest. It's like planting a seed that grows over time, providing financial security. Learning about investment options opens up opportunities for your money to work for you. Investing in stocks or bonds can potentially yield higher returns than a savings account, though it's important to understand the associated risks. Educating yourself on investment basics allows you to make informed decisions, potentially increasing your wealth over time.

Numerous resources are available for those eager to enhance their financial literacy. Financial literacy courses offer structured learning on managing money, understanding investments, and planning for the future.

These courses can be found online or through community education programs, providing flexibility in learning. Online budgeting tools simplify the process of managing finances, offering features like automated tracking, expense categorization, and goal setting. These tools act as personal financial advisors, guiding you toward smarter financial decisions and greater independence. With the proper knowledge, you can confidently negotiate the economic landscape, turning what might seem like a maze into a well-lit path toward financial independence and security.

EMBRACING INDEPENDENCE: SETTING AND ACHIEVING PERSONAL GOALS

Now, you stand at the start of a new path, with each step forward shaped by your ambitions and dreams. Setting personal goals is like mapping out this path, offering direction and purpose in your journey toward independence. Goals motivate and guide personal development, acting as beacons that light the way. It is important to distinguish between long-term and short-term goals. Short-term goals are like stepping stones, achievable within weeks or months, while long-term goals stretch further into the horizon, requiring sustained effort that can take years. Both types serve a significant role, with short-term goals providing quick wins that build confidence and long-term goals offering a vision to strive towards.

To create meaningful and attainable objectives, employing goal-setting frameworks can be incredibly helpful. The SMART goals method is a popular choice, emphasizing objectives that are Specific, Measurable, Achievable, Relevant, and Time-bound. What if your goal is to improve your artistic skills? Instead of a vague aim like "get better at drawing," a SMART goal would be "complete a drawing course within three months." This level of specific detail provides clarity and a timeline, making the goal more tangible. Vision boards also serve as powerful resources for goal visualization. By creating a collage of images and words representing your aspirations, you manifest your dreams visually, keeping motivation high and direction clear.

Tracking progress and celebrating achievements are major aspects of the goal-setting process. Keeping a goal-tracking journal allows you to document your journey, noting each milestone reached and reflecting on the lessons learned along the way. This practice not only maintains focus but also provides a touchable record of growth. Reward systems for milestones achieved can further motivate you to persevere. Whether treating yourself to a favorite activity or celebrating with friends, acknowledging successes reinforces positive behavior and encourages continued effort.

Having clear objectives, combined with a structured approach, can turn your dreams into reality. By setting and pursuing personal goals, you harness your potential, leading the way for growth and independence. Whether the goals are personal, academic, or professional, they offer a framework for success, guiding you toward a future that aligns with your passions and ambitions.

As we close this chapter, remember that each goal set is a step towards self-discovery and independence. Next, we will explore the emotional and mental well-being of teens on the spectrum, providing insights and strategies to support a balanced and healthy life.

7

EMOTIONAL AND MENTAL WELL-BEING

I magine a world where your mind is a bustling city with no traffic lights, and every thought is a different vehicle trying to speed through intersections without colliding. This is what managing stress and emotions can feel like for many teens with autism. The constant noise and movement can be overwhelming, leaving you yearning for a moment of peace. Enter meditation, a practice that offers those much-needed traffic lights, helping to regulate the chaos and bring a sense of calm. Meditation is not just for monks on mountaintops; it's a resource accessible to everyone, offering a pathway to inner peace, even amidst the hustle and bustle of daily life.

Meditation has been suggested as a worthwhile practice for those with autism, offering relaxation and improved social quality of life. It can reduce stress and even help with physical regulation through techniques like breathing exercises. The beauty of meditation lies in its simplicity and accessibility; you don't need special equipment or a serene setting to begin. You can start right where you are, whether it's a quiet room at home or a busy school library. The goal is to find a practice that fits into your life, providing a mental sanctuary where you can retreat and recharge.

Let's start with guided imagery exercises, a gentle way to introduce meditation. Picture yourself lying on a beach, the sun warming your skin as the waves kiss the shore. Or perhaps you're walking through a forest, the scent of pine in the air and the sound of leaves crunching beneath your feet. Guided imagery exercises invite you on a sensory journey, allowing your mind to wander to places of tranquility and comfort. These exercises can be led by a recording or a supportive guide, helping to create a vivid mental landscape where stress dissolves like morning fog.

Breathing exercises offer another avenue to inner peace and can be practiced anywhere. Focus on your breath, the gentle rise and fall of your chest, the cool air entering your nostrils, and the warmth as it leaves. This focus acts as an anchor, pulling you back to the present moment and away from the whirlpool of anxious thoughts. A simple technique is the 4-7-8 method: inhale for four seconds, hold for seven, and exhale for eight. This rhythmic pattern helps slow your heart rate and calm your nervous system, making it a powerful method for stress reduction.

Body scan meditation is a practice that encourages you to tune into your physical self, enhancing the connection between mind and body. Start by lying down in a comfortable position, closing your eyes, and taking a few deep breaths. Begin at the top of your head and slowly work your way down to your toes, paying attention to each part of your body. Notice any tension, discomfort, or sensation, and consciously relax those areas. This practice promotes self-awareness and relaxation, helping to release stress stored in your muscles.

CREATING YOUR MEDITATION ROUTINE

Consider setting aside a few minutes daily to experiment with different meditation techniques. Reflect on which practices resonate with you and note how they affect your mood and stress levels. This reflection can help you develop a personalized meditation routine specific to your unique needs and preferences. There's no right or wrong way to meditate. The goal is to discover what brings you peace and include it in your daily life.

Meditation is a practice that grows with time, becoming more rewarding as you devote more of your schedule to it. Meditation is a great option for everyone—teens, parents, and educators alike—offering a moment of serenity in our often chaotic lives. By embracing meditation, you open the door to a calmer, more centered self, ready to face the world with renewed energy and tranquility.

RECOGNIZING BURNOUT: SIGNS AND PREVENTION
STRATEGIES

Is there anything more aggravating than a smartphone that just won't hold a charge? No matter how long you plug in, you never quite reach 100%. That's what burnout can feel like—a persistent state of exhaustion that no amount of rest seems to cure. For teens on the spectrum, burnout is often the result of chronic stress, unrealistic demands, and the relentless need to mask their true selves in a world that doesn't always understand them. This exhaustion isn't just physical; it also seeps into emotions and performance. You might find yourself too tired to engage in activities you once loved or struggling to focus on schoolwork that used to come easily. Emotional exhaustion can make you feel detached or irritable, and reduced performance can lead to a frustrating cycle of self-doubt.

Spotting the signs of burnout early is essential. Chronic fatigue is more than just being tired after a late night; it's a weariness that doesn't go away with sleep. Emotional exhaustion may reveal itself as feeling overwhelmed by even small tasks or losing interest in things that once brought joy. Reduced performance can result in slipping grades, missed deadlines, or a general lack of motivation. These signs can be subtle at first, like a whisper of wind before a storm, but recognizing them is the first step to preventing burnout from taking hold.

Preventing burnout requires setting realistic expectations. It's easy to fall into the trap of thinking we need to be perfect at everything —school, friendships, hobbies—but perfection is an illusion. Instead, focus on what's achievable. Break tasks into smaller, more manageable steps and celebrate each small victory. It's okay to ask for help or say no to overwhelming things. Prioritizing rest and relaxation is essential, too. Schedule downtime just like you would any other commitment. Whether it's reading a book, taking a walk, or simply daydreaming, these moments of calm mean everything when it comes to recharging your internal battery.

We mentioned boundaries earlier. Setting boundaries plays a crucial role in keeping burnout at bay. In a world that often demands more than we can give, learning to say no is a super-power. This might mean declining an invitation to yet another social event or limiting extracurricular activities to focus on personal interests. Allocating time for yourself isn't selfish—it's necessary. By creating a balance between obligations and relax-ation, you can protect your mental health and maintain your well-being.

Consider the story of Mia, a high school student who was juggling academics, a part-time job, and the demands of social life. At first, she ignored the signs of burnout, pushing through the fatigue and emotional turmoil. But when her grades began to slip, she realized something had to change. With the support of her family and teachers, Mia started setting boundaries. She prioritized her commitments, cut back on work hours, and scheduled regular breaks in her day. Gradually, she regained her energy and enthusi-asm, finding a rhythm that worked for her. Mia's story is a testa-ment to the power of boundaries and balance in overcoming burnout.

Rebalancing work and life often involves reassessing priorities. You have to figure out what truly matters ,and don't be afraid to let go of the rest. This might mean focusing more on quality relation-ships rather than quantity or choosing activities that bring joy rather than stress. It's a personal experience unique to each indi-vidual. For some, it might involve taking up a new hobby or reconnecting with nature. For others, it could mean seeking professional support to negotiate the complexities of burnout. Whatever it may be, the goal is to create a sustainable and fulfilling life where burnout has no room to succeed.

CREATIVE OUTLETS: ART, MUSIC, AND SELF-EXPRESSION

For many teens with autism, creative outlets like art and music serve as vital channels for expression and emotional release. Every stroke of a paintbrush and every note played on a guitar tells a story that their words sometimes fail to express. They provide a safe space where feelings can flow freely without the constraints of conventional communication. Art therapy, for instance, allows individuals to translate their emotions into colors and shapes, offering insights into their inner worlds that might otherwise remain hidden. The canvas becomes a trusted friend, listening without judgment and reflecting back the complexities of the artist's feelings.

Music therapy, on the other hand, taps into the profound connection between rhythm and mood regulation. Strumming a guitar or tapping a drum can create a sense of order and predictability, soothing the chaos that sometimes swirls in the mind. The vibrations resonate deep within, creating harmony in both sound and spirit. This therapeutic engagement with music can stabilize emotions, helping to manage stress and anxiety. Whether it's the structured repetition of a favorite melody or the spontaneous creation of new songs, music therapy can be a powerful outlet for teens with autism.

Exploring different creative outlets opens doors to a multitude of self-expression opportunities. Painting and drawing, for instance, provide a tactile and visual medium to explore emotions. Each brushstroke or pencil line carries a piece of the artist's soul, capturing moments of joy, sadness, or introspection. Writing poetry or short stories offers another avenue where words express narratives that give voice to thoughts and dreams. These literary creations can be a cathartic release, allowing for reflection and processing of experiences. Playing musical instruments, from the piano's harmonious chords to the violin's soulful notes, invites a physical connection to sound, where each note played is a step toward self-discovery and expression.

Creativity is pivotal in self-discovery, acting as a mirror reflecting the artist's essence. Through journaling, individuals can embark on a journey of self-reflection, where words flow freely, unburdened by the need for external validation. This practice encourages introspection, helping to uncover personal truths and insights. The act of creating itself becomes a dialogue with the self, fostering growth and understanding. It's a process that invites exploration, where mistakes are simply part of the learning curve, and every creation is a testament to personal growth.

A CANVAS FOR EMOTIONAL HEALTH

Consider collaborative art installations where individuals contribute their unique pieces to a larger work of art. These projects celebrate community, showcasing how different perspectives can come together to create something beautiful. Community music performances offer another opportunity to share creativity with others. Whether it's a school band concert or a neighborhood talent show, performing music in a group setting promotes connection and mutual support. These projects provide platforms for creative expression and build confidence and a sense of belonging.

Engaging in creative outlets is a pathway to emotional well-being and self-discovery. Each stroke of paint, each note played, or word written is a step towards understanding and acceptance. By embracing creativity, teens on the spectrum can explore their identities, express their emotions, and connect with the world in ways that are uniquely their own.

PHYSICAL HEALTH: THE CONNECTION BETWEEN BODY AND MIND

When your physical health is nurtured, your mental well-being often follows suit, creating a balance that enhances your overall quality of life. One of the most significant aspects of maintaining this balance is exercise. Regular physical activity helps the body to reduce anxiety and stress. When you move your body, your brain releases endorphins, those wonderful chemicals that lift your mood and create a sense of calm. Exercise doesn't have to mean intense gym sessions or running marathons. It can be as simple as dancing to your favorite song in the living room or taking a leisurely stroll through your neighborhood. These activities benefit your body and provide a mental escape, a chance to clear your mind and focus on the present.

Maintaining physical health involves more than just exercise; it requires a holistic approach that includes balanced nutrition and adequate sleep. Think of your body as a car that needs the right fuel to run smoothly. Eating a variety of foods ensures you get the nutrients needed to support both physical and mental functions. Incorporate colorful fruits and vegetables, lean proteins, and whole grains into your meals to keep your energy levels stable and your mind sharp. Sleep is equally important, acting as your body's nightly tune-up. During sleep, your body repairs itself and your brain processes the day's events. Establish a routine that allows for consistent sleep, aiming for seven to nine hours each night. Create a calming bedtime ritual, like reading or listening to soothing music, to signal to your body that it's time to wind down.

Outdoor activities offer an additional layer of benefits for your emotional health. Nature has a unique way of soothing the soul, providing a backdrop of serenity that invites reflection and relaxation. Walking through a park or hiking a trail immerses you in the sights and sounds of the natural world, offering a break from the hustle of daily life. The fresh air and sunlight can boost your mood and provide a sense of peace that indoor environments often lack. Engaging in outdoor sports, whether it's a casual game of soccer or a round of Frisbee, combines the benefits of physical activity with the joy of being outside.

Small changes can lead to substantial improvements. This should encourage you to explore what types of physical activities resonate with you. Whether it's yoga, cycling, or a simple walk in the park, finding what you enjoy can be the key to sustaining an active lifestyle that supports both body and mind.

Physical health is a natural part of overall well-being. By nurturing your body through exercise, nutrition, and outdoor activities, you create a foundation that supports mental health. This holistic approach enables you to take charge of your well-being, creating a harmonious balance that enhances your quality of life.

THERAPY AND COUNSELING: FINDING THE RIGHT SUPPORT

Teens on the spectrum can struggle with emotions and social dynamics. Sometimes, they feel like they are attempting to solve a word problem where a sentence or two is missing. Therapy and counseling can provide the missing information. Engaging with a therapist can feel like having a conversation with a wise friend who's seen it all. They listen without judgment and offer insights that illuminate the path ahead. Therapy can help untangle complex emotions, build resilience, and develop strategies for handling stress and anxiety.

Exploring the types of therapy available can help you find the right fit. Cognitive-behavioral therapy (CBT) focuses on identifying and changing negative thought patterns, offering practical strategies to manage anxiety and depression. It's like reprogramming a computer to run more efficiently, eliminating glitches that slow down progress. Dialectical behavior therapy (DBT) emphasizes mindfulness and emotional regulation, teaching skills to manage intense emotions and improve relationships. It's similar to learning a new language that helps you communicate more effectively with yourself and others. For those who find solace in creativity, art and music therapy provide avenues to express emotions non-verbally. These therapies tap into the power of creativity, allowing individuals to explore their inner worlds through color, sound, and movement.

Finding the right therapist is crucial for a positive experience. Start by researching therapist qualifications, ensuring they have the expertise and experience to address your specific needs. Look for credentials such as licensure and specialized training in working with teens with autism. Initial consultations can be a helpful way to gauge compatibility. Consider it a test drive, where you get to experience the therapist's style and approach. During this meeting, don't hesitate to ask questions about their methods and how they plan to support your goals. Remember, therapy is a collaboration, and finding someone you feel comfortable with can make all the difference.

Different therapeutic approaches offer unique benefits tailored to individual needs. CBT, for example, is widely used for its effectiveness in treating anxiety and depression. By challenging negative thoughts and beliefs, it enables individuals to take control of their mental health. DBT, on the other hand, is particularly helpful for those experiencing intense emotions. It provides devices to negotiate emotional storms, bringing a sense of calm and balance. Art and music therapy engage the senses, offering a non-verbal outlet for expression. These therapies can be especially helpful for those who struggle with traditional talk therapy, providing an alternative way to communicate and process emotions.

Choosing therapy is a step towards enhancing what's already inside you, helping build a more fulfilling and balanced life. Therapy offers a space to explore, learn, and grow with a supportive guide by your side. Whether it's through talk, art, or music, the right therapeutic approach can open doors to new possibilities, increasing resilience and emotional well-being.

SELF-CARE RITUALS: DAILY PRACTICES FOR EMOTIONAL HEALTH

Self-care is designed to help maintain your emotional health and well-being. Self-care isn't just a trendy buzzword; it's a vital practice that involves taking time to nurture yourself, both physically and emotionally. You should take the time to recognize your needs and then take steps to meet them. Daily self-care routines are like a foundation for your mental health, offering stability during life's ups and downs. Think of these routines as small acts of kindness you extend to yourself, reminding you that your well-being is a priority.

Including self-care in your daily life can be both rewarding and enjoyable. Start by exploring activities that resonate with you personally.

Engaging in hobbies and interests can provide a sense of accomplishment and joy. Whether it's painting, gardening, or even building model airplanes, these activities offer a break from daily stressors, allowing your mind to focus and recharge. Journaling exercises are another excellent way to process emotions and reflect on your day. By putting pen to paper, you create a space to explore your thoughts without judgment, gaining an understanding of your feelings and experiences.

Gratitude practices, though simple, can have profound effects on your outlook. Taking a moment each day to acknowledge the positive aspects of your life can shift your focus from what's lacking to what you appreciate. This practice doesn't need to be elaborate. It could be as simple as writing down three things you're grateful for each night before bed. Over time, these small acknowledgments can build a more optimistic perspective, helping you handle challenges that come your way.

The role of self-care in stress management is significant. Regular self-care can act as a buffer against stress, reducing its impact on your mental and physical health. Establishing a self-care schedule guarantees that you prioritize these practices, much like scheduling a meeting or appointment. It could be a ten-minute morning meditation, an afternoon stroll, or a relaxing evening bath. The key is consistency—making self-care a non-negotiable part of your routine. This commitment to yourself reinforces the message that your well-being matters, leading to a healthier, more balanced life.

The beauty of self-care lies in its flexibility. Some days, you might need the solitude of a quiet walk, while others call for the companionship of a friend. The goal is to listen to your needs and respond with kindness and intention. Doing so creates a supportive environment for yourself, nurturing emotional health and resilience. Self-care is not an indulgence; it's a necessity, a way to recharge and reconnect with yourself among the demands of life. As you continue to explore and refine your self-care practices, remember that every small step towards nurturing yourself is a step towards a healthier, more fulfilling life.

8

CELEBRATING AND EMPOWERING TEENS WITH AUTISM

T he lights go down in a crowded auditorium. You step onto the stage, spotlight beaming down, as you prepare to share your story with the world. For many teens with autism, finding their voice and place in the world can feel just like stepping into that spotlight. This chapter is dedicated to shining a light on those who have taken the stage and made a significant difference. Their stories not only inspire but also illustrate the limitless potential that lies within each individual on the spectrum. Let's explore the lives of some remarkable individuals who have created their own paths and achieved greatness, offering us all a ray of hope and possibility.

INDIVIDUALS WITH AUTISM WHO MADE A DIFFERENCE

Temple Grandin's story is full of innovation and resilience. Diagnosed with autism at a time when the condition was surrounded by misunderstanding, Grandin saw the world through a unique lens—literally thinking in pictures. This perspective allowed her to revolutionize animal science, designing humane livestock systems that have improved the welfare of countless animals. Her curved chute system is evidence of her ability to transform her challenges into strengths, challenging a male-dominated industry and advocating for neurodiversity. Grandin's journey highlights how embracing one's differences can lead to profound contributions, both in her field and in changing how the entire world looks at autism. Her legacy is a powerful reminder that what makes us different can also be our greatest strength.

Greta Thunberg, a name synonymous with environmental activism, has shown the world the power of unwavering focus and clarity. Diagnosed with Asperger's Syndrome, Thunberg refers to her autism as her "superpower," which has fueled her commitment to fighting climate change. Her "school strike for climate" movement ignited a global youth activism wave, proving that one voice can lead to monumental change, no matter how young or different. Thunberg challenges stereotypes by standing as a symbol of empowerment, using her platform to promote neurodiversity and advocate for urgent environmental action. Her story inspires teen on the spectrum to embrace their unique perspectives and use them to make a difference.

The impact of these stories extends beyond individual achievements; they offer a sense of representation and visibility in media that is often lacking. Seeing successful individuals with autism in prominent roles provides a mirror for teens to see themselves and their potential. These stories encourage you to pursue your passions, whether they align with science, activism, or any other field. They show that you can overcome barriers and achieve your dreams with persistence and dedication. The common traits shared among successful individuals on the spectrum, such as resilience and problem-solving abilities, are skills that can be nurtured and developed over time. These stories illustrate that success isn't about fitting into a mold but about shaping the world around you.

For teens looking to draw inspiration from these role models, consider setting personal goals that resonate with your passions and interests. Whether you find motivation in Temple Grandin's innovative spirit or Greta Thunberg's activism, use their stories to chart your own course. Engaging in mentorship programs can also provide guidance and support as you begin your own course. Mentors can offer insights and encouragement, helping you develop the skills and confidence needed to achieve your goals.

SETTING YOUR OWN GOALS

Take a moment to reflect on what you are passionate about. What are your interests, and how can you use them to make an impact? Write down a few goals inspired by the stories of Temple Grandin and Greta Thunberg or anyone else who has had an influence on your life. Consider seeking out a mentor who shares your interests and can guide you along the way. This exercise encourages you to think about your future and the steps you can take to achieve your dreams.

THE ROLE OF NEURODIVERSITY: EMBRACING DIFFERENT WAYS OF THINKING

The most beautiful and visually impressive gardens are filled with various plants, each with its unique color, shape, and fragrance. This is how we can visualize the concept of neurodiversity—a celebration of the diverse ways in which human brains function. Neurodiversity embraces neurological differences, including autism, as natural variations in the human genome. It recognizes that these differences enrich our communities, much like the diverse flora in a garden. Acceptance of neurological diversity is important for creating an inclusive society where everyone has the opportunity to succeed. It challenges the outdated notion that there is only one "correct" way to think or learn.

In this context, focusing on the strengths of individuals with autism becomes the leading factor. Teens on the spectrum often possess unique problem-solving skills that can offer fresh perspectives. They're known for their ability to think outside the box and find innovative solutions to complex issues. Creativity and innovation are also common traits, with many individuals excelling in artistic and scientific fields. By highlighting these strengths, we shift the story from what individuals with autism can't do to what they can achieve. This strengths-focused viewpoint allows teens to pursue their passions and develop their talents, leading to personal fulfillment and contributions to society.

The benefits of diverse thinking extend beyond individual achievements. In society, different ways of thinking contribute to innovation in technology, arts, and sciences. Many technological advancements have been driven by those who view the world slightly differently from everyone else. Individuals with autism often bring unparalleled attention to detail and a knack for identifying patterns, skills that are highly sought after in fields like coding, engineering, and design. In the arts, their creativity can lead to groundbreaking works that challenge traditional perspectives. By embracing neurodiversity, we open the door to many new ideas and innovations that enrich our world.

Educational settings play an instrumental role in developing this acceptance and understanding. By working neurodiversity into teaching practices, educators can create inclusive environments where all students can succeed. Creating an inclusive curriculum means considering the diverse needs of learners and providing multiple ways to access information. This might involve using visual aids, hands-on activities, or technology to accommodate different learning styles. Peer education programs can also be helpful in promoting understanding and compassion among students. By educating all students about neurodiversity, schools can create a culture of acceptance and support where differences are celebrated rather than criticized.

NEURODIVERSITY AWARENESS ACTIVITY

Consider organizing a Neurodiversity Awareness Week at your school or community center. Include activities like workshops, guest speakers, and interactive sessions that highlight the strengths of neurodiverse individuals. Encourage students to share their experiences and talents. This initiative can serve as a platform for teens on the spectrum to showcase their abilities and educate others about the value of neurodiversity. It's an opportunity to build bridges of understanding and create a more inclusive community where everyone feels valued and empowered to contribute their unique talents.

APPLYING STRENGTHS: TURNING CHALLENGES INTO ADVANTAGES

For teens with autism, recognizing their individual strengths is the key to personal growth and development. Strengths-based assessments can help you identify these abilities, offering a structured way to understand what makes you exceptional. These assessments provide insights into your natural talents and how they can be nurtured. Personal reflection exercises can also play a vital role, allowing you to explore your interests and passions in a meaningful way. By taking the time to reflect, you can begin to see the patterns in your strengths and how they can be applied to various areas of your life.

Once you have identified these strengths, the next step is learning how to leverage them in practical ways. For example, a strengths-based learning approach can be instrumental in education. This method focuses on using your strengths to overcome challenges rather than trying to fit into a one-size-fits-all educational model. If you're a visual learner, including visual aids and tools can enhance your understanding and retention of information. Similarly, aligning your path with your personal talents can lead to fulfillment and success in your career. Whether you have a knack for technology or a passion for the arts, finding a career that resonates with your strengths allows you to excel in an environment that values your unique contributions.

While seemingly frightening, challenges can become growth opportunities when looked at the right way. Turning setbacks into learning experiences is a powerful strategy. Instead of seeing a mistake as a failure, consider it a stepping stone toward improvement. This mindset encourages resilience and adaptability, essential traits for handling life's ups and downs. Developing adaptive strategies helps you tackle challenges head-on, turning potential obstacles into advantages. For instance, if you struggle with social interactions, practicing in a comfortable setting can build confidence and improve your skills over time. It's about finding what works for you and using that knowledge to confidently overcome challenges.

Entrepreneurs often draw from their unique perspectives to innovate and create solutions that others might overlook. Their ability to think outside the box and approach problems creatively sets them apart. Artists, too, channel their sensory experiences into their work, creating pieces that resonate on a deeply emotional level. These individuals have learned to embrace their differences, using them as a vehicle for success. Their stories serve as a reminder that by leveraging your strengths, you can achieve remarkable things.

IDENTIFYING YOUR STRENGTHS

Take a moment to reflect on what makes you unique. What are your strengths, and how have they helped you in the past? Consider writing down a few examples of times when you've used your strengths to overcome a challenge or achieve a goal. This exercise can provide valuable insights into how you can continue to apply your strengths in the future.

ENCOURAGING TALENTS THROUGH CREATIVITY

Creativity is like a key that unlocks hidden doors within us, doors that lead to new worlds of self-expression and communication. For teens with autism, creative pursuits offer a personal way to express thoughts and emotions that sometimes escape words. Whether through painting, music, or writing, these outlets allow you to communicate the distinction of your inner world in vibrant, physical ways. Engaging in creative activities can serve as a therapeutic escape, providing a safe space to explore feelings and ideas without judgment. This process is liberating and helpful for mental health, as it can reduce stress and create a sense of accomplishment. Art, for instance, can transcend verbal barriers, enabling you to convey complex emotions through color and form. With its rhythms and melodies, music can tell stories and evoke withindeep emotions. These creative expressions expand your ability to communicate, offering new avenues for connection and understanding.

Nurturing your creative talents requires intentional effort and exploration. Enrolling in art or music classes is a great way to sharpen your skills and meet others who share your interests. These classes provide structured learning, allowing you to experiment with different techniques and mediums. Participating in creative workshops or local community events can also offer inspiration and opportunities to collaborate with other teens. Workshops often focus on specific skills, such as songwriting or digital art, and can ignite new passions. Beyond formal settings, the internet is a great place to find all kinds of resources, from tutorials to forums where you can learn and share your work with a global audience. Creativity is a journey, not a destination, where you continue to explore what excites you and find joy in the process of creating.

Creativity enhances self-expression and also improves problem-solving skills. When you engage in creative thinking, you develop the ability to see challenges from different angles and devise innovative solutions. Brainstorming sessions, for example, encourage free thinking and the exploration of unconventional ideas. This approach can lead to breakthroughs, whether you're tackling a complex math problem or constructing a new game strategy.

CONCLUSION

As we come to the end of "Teen Autism Essentials," I hope you find yourself armed with new understanding, practical strategies, and a heart full of empathy. We've covered a lot of ground together, from understanding the vibrant spectrum of autism in adolescence to building emotional intelligence and advocating for oneself. We've walked alongside parents, offering them support and guidance, and we've equipped educators with devices to create inclusive classrooms. We've looked into the social dynamics that shape teenage years, prepared for the thrilling leap into adulthood, and emphasized the importance of emotional well-being. And finally, we've celebrated the unique strengths and limitless potential of teens on the spectrum.

This book was born from a vision to offer a comprehensive and inspiring guide for teens with autism, their parents, and educators. I wanted to provide more than just information. I aimed to deliver useful strategies, share uplifting stories, and offer a fresh perspective on autism. My goal is to embrace the uniqueness of each individual and make room for everyone to succeed. I hope you've found this book to be a beacon of light, a companion on your journey, and a source of empowerment.

As you finish the final pages, let me leave you with some key takeaways. Embrace neurodiversity as a strength, not a challenge. Celebrate the different ways we think, learn, and connect. Remember the power of self-advocacy—it opens doors to personal independence and fulfillment. Recognize the importance of community support; no one should walk this path alone. And always hold onto the belief that teens with autism can lead fulfilling, impactful lives, filled with joy and purpose.

Now, here's my call to action for you. For teens, embrace your individual strengths. Pursue your passions with energy and confidence. You have so much to offer the world, and your voice matters. For parents, continue to support and advocate for your children. Stand by them as they sort through the complexities of adolescence and beyond. For educators, strive to create inclusive environments where every student feels valued and understood. Your role is crucial in shaping a future where diversity is celebrated.

I want to inspire hope and confidence as we part ways. The road is not always easy, but it's filled with potential for growth, independence, and positive impact. The autism community is vibrant and resilient, and together, we can achieve remarkable things. Let us continue to challenge stereotypes, build bridges of understanding, and celebrate the beauty of neurodiversity.

This is not the end but rather a stepping stone for continued learning and exploration. I encourage you to seek out resources, engage with communities, and look for opportunities for both personal and communal growth. The world is filled with possibilities, and your journey doesn't stop here. Keep asking questions, keep pushing boundaries, and keep learning.

I owe a debt of gratitude to all those who have contributed to this book. The individuals who shared their stories and insights, the community that offered unwavering support, and the collaboration that made this book possible. Thank you for being part of this with me. Your experiences and wisdom have been invaluable.

On a personal note, I want to remind any teens reading this that I was once exactly where you were. I was the new kid at three different schools, but I eventually found my people. Over 25 years after graduating, I still have friends from high school. With time and patience, you will find your people if you haven't already. Thank you for allowing me to be part of your experience. The story doesn't end here. It's just the beginning.

REFERENCES

American Academy of Pediatrics. (2023). *Affirming care for autism and gender diversity.* *Pediatrics, 152*(2), e2023061813. https://publications.aap.org/pediatrics/article/152/2/e2023061813/192500/Affirming-Care-for-Autism-and-Gender-Diversity

Applied Behavioral Training and Applied Behavior Analysis. (n.d.). *Puberty and autism: An unexplored transition.* ABTABA Blog. https://www.abtaba.com/blog/puberty-and-autism

Association of American Colleges & Universities. (n.d.). *Neurodiversity is diversity.* https://www.aacu.org/liberaleducation/articles/neurodiversity-is-diversity

Autism Parenting Magazine. (n.d.). *Autism success stories: Independence and work.* https://www.autismparentingmagazine.com/success-stories-independence-work

Autism Parenting Magazine. (n.d.). *Social anxiety in autism: All you need to know.* https://www.autismparentingmagazine.com/social-anxiety-through-mom-eyes/

Autism Speaks. (n.d.). *Autism and exercise: Special benefits.* https://www.autismspeaks.org/expert-opinion/autism-exercise-benefits

Children's Hospital of Philadelphia. (n.d.). *Therapeutic role-playing games for autistic individuals.* https://www.research.chop.edu/therapeutic-role-playing-games-for-autistic-individuals

Harbor School. (2022). *The 7 essential life skills for those with autism.* https://harborschool.com/2022/01/19/the-7-essential-life-skills-for-those-with-autism/

Hands Center. (n.d.). *9 sensory-friendly home modifications for autism.* https://www.handscenter.com/9-sensory-friendly-home-modifications-for-autism#:.

Hope for Three. (n.d.). *Empowering autistic children for financial independence.* https://hopeforthree.org/empowering-autistic-children-for-financial-independence/

Level Ahead ABA. (n.d.). *Understanding Greta Thunberg's autism journey and impact.* https://www.levelaheadaba.com/blog/greta-thunberg-autism#:~:text=How%20has%20Thunberg's%20autism%20influenced,voice%20in%20the%20environmental%20movement.

Middletown Autism Resource. (n.d.). *Boundaries: Public, private, personal space.* https://teenage-resource.middletownautism.com/teenage-issues-and-strategies/relationships-and-sexuality/relationships/boundaries-public-private-personal-space/

Middletown Autism Resource. (n.d.). *Teaching empathy and reciprocity - Building capacity resource.* https://capacity-resource.middletownautism.com/strategies/supporting-the-individual-with-autism/teaching-empathy-and-reciprocity/

National Autistic Society. (n.d.). Understanding autistic burnout. https://www.autism.org.uk/advice-and-guidance/professional-practice/autistic-burnout

National Center for Biotechnology Information. (n.d.). Meditation as a potential therapy for autism: A review. PMC. https://pmc.ncbi.nlm.nih.gov/articles/PMC3420737/

National Center for Biotechnology Information. (n.d.). Music therapy for people with autism spectrum disorder. PMC. https://pmc.ncbi.nlm.nih.gov/articles/PMC6956617/#:~

National Center for Biotechnology Information. (n.d.). Short report: The role of parental advocacy in addressing... PMC. https://pmc.ncbi.nlm.nih.gov/articles/PMC9010347/

National University. (n.d.). 7 autism behavior and communication strategies. https://www.nu.edu/blog/7-autism-behavior-and-communication-strategies/

New Focus Academy. (n.d.). Nonverbal communication in teens with autism. https://newfocusacademy.com/nonverbal-communication-in-teens-with-autism/

Rainbow Therapy. (n.d.). How to manage stress and anxiety in autism. https://www.rainbowtherapy.org/bloghow-to-manage-stress-and-anxiety-in-autism/

Raising Children Network. (n.d.). Sensory sensitivities: Autistic children and teenagers. https://raisingchildren.net.au/autism/behaviour/understanding-behaviour/sensory-sensitivities-asd

Reading Rockets. (n.d.). Supporting students with autism: 10 ideas for inclusive classrooms. https://www.readingrockets.org/topics/autism-spectrum-disorder/articles/supporting-students-autism-10-ideas-inclusive-classrooms

Reading Rockets. (n.d.). Visual supports for students with ASD. https://www.readingrockets.org/topics/autism-spectrum-disorder/articles/visual-supports-students-asd

Rock and Art Museum. (n.d.). Temple Grandin: Innovator in animal science and autism. https://www.rockandart.org/temple-grandin-animal-science-and-autism/

Stages Learning. (n.d.). Helping your autistic child develop emotional intelligence. https://blog.stageslearning.com/blog/helping-your-autistic-child-develop-emotional-intelligence

Stages Learning. (n.d.). Support groups for autistic children, teens, young adults, and parents. https://blog.stageslearning.com/blog/support-groups-for-autistic-children-teens-young-adults-and-parents

The Autism Community in Action. (n.d.). Self-advocacy. https://tacanow.org/family-resources/self-advocacy/

ThinkWork. (n.d.). Career development for youth with autism spectrum disorder. https://www.thinkwork.org/considering-community-service-career-development-youth-autism-spectrum-disorder

University of Minnesota. (n.d.). The autism mentorship program (AMP): Addressing mental health and social isolation among autistic youth. CURA. https://www.cura.umn.edu/research/autism-mentorship-program-amp-addressing-mental-health-and-social-isolation-among-autistic

WebMD. (n.d.). *Autism myths and facts*. WebMD. *https://www.webmd.com/brain/autism/features/autism-myths-facts*

Wikipedia. (n.d.). *Stephen Wiltshire*. *https://en.wikipedia.org/wiki/Stephen_Wiltshire#:*